The Big Event, Lost Notes, or Insecurities

By

Andrew Therriault

Printed in the United States of America

First Printing, 2021

ISBN 978-1-7338944-7-0

www.AndrewTherriaultBooks.com

Part 1

The Serious Event

Chapter 1

There is now more to the situation that can help us reach a conclusion, and there is now another book that is well part of the conclusion. That part, which should be undisclosed, to the pain before and after the ordeal…

Resuming one summer morning: walking into a building, readjusting, unnerved, unsettled. I opened the door and there was someone in the lobby behind the counter. I asked, "Excuse me, sir, I don't have my room key, I lost my cell phone, my car died overnight, can you help me?"

"Oh, of course," he said.

He seemed taken aback. He is a kind, generous person; whereas, at that moment, I was quite dazed and daunted. Sitting down at the table, I rubbed my eyes, smelled hot coffee. Then, after readjusting, giving or getting a moment, another second passed and a steaming cup was on the table, and the clerk sat down behind the counter. He asked, "What happened last night?"

"What, I don't know."

I sipped the coffee, again, again, and the thoughts came back, some memories came back, a little bit of everything came back; where I am, what had happened, what to do. What to do…

I had arrived in New Orleans the previous day. I first got gas at a local gas station. Then I drove very slowly, following the traffic, through the streets. And then on Ursuline Street I parked in front of the hotel. My car, The Honda, did shut off, but not completely. The engine shut off; the power stayed on. At least the air conditioner did, that stayed on, and so did other features, like the display screens and the fan. All of these stayed on, while the engine and the rest of the car shut off. At first, in that moment, it was hardly a concern. But before even getting out of the car, I called Honda support. A woman from New York answered, and after a cordial greeting, then telling her about the problem, she said that if in the morning the problem persists, take it to a dealership and they will fix it in the garage. I listened, remembered, and then toward the end of her explanation on what else to do, the call was disconnected. But what more was there to expect? I had been on the road for four days straight, and The Honda drove smoothly all that time two thousand miles with no problems, and there was no reason to be concerned that this observation would turn into a problem. It was a newer car, The Honda, and I thought that the power would just keep running, keep going. Plus, I thought that if it became a problem, worst-case scenario, I would only have to bring it to a dealership and then the problem would be resolved. Really, I had been driving all day, and I wanted to get out of the car and explore the French Quarter.

I pressed the start button again and the engine turned on; everything in the car was on. Then I pressed the stop button and only the engine shut off. I felt the soft flow of air from the fan, and I saw on the screen that the power was on—still.

I thought, well, I will just check on it later. Fingers crossed it will still be on. Call for assistance otherwise.

The check-in at the hotel was quick. Just down the hall past the lobby was a courtyard. There the sun sat overhead and on the ground were several small puddles, chairs, tables, a few fountains. There were many plants of the tropical variety, perhaps banana trees, but not the kind with fruit, the kind with only their appealing green leaves. My room had one of these plants right outside the door, next to a chair, in the sun. I went inside, showered, changed, and then went outside and down the street for a walk.

It seemed like over time the history of the neighborhood had been preserved very well. Hardly anything seemed altered from its original form. It had that character still. And that liveliness. And there was a bit of mystery in the air, maybe a bit of sorcery that almost seemed natural there, and unique. Mix that with folklore, spirits, hauntings, parties, crimes, past and present. Also, the blue sky and the sun, the mid-day rain, the smell of seafood, soup, spices; the sound of saxophones, kids drumming on buckets, nicely.

"You're very good at that," I said.

"How about some money."

I gave him what I went out with. It was not much. But after all, at that moment, I had my debit card *and* credit card. I walked away toward the city, and he started drumming again, amid the bustle, louder than ever.

There are certain foods, I had recently learned, that I cannot or rather should not consume. This includes certain vegetables, fruits, spices, grains, sweeteners, et cetera. I will have to explain this more effectively later on; it's part of the insecurities. But for now, I will say that consuming something with any of those ingredients causes abdominal discomfort, and often pain, very much affecting the quality of life. So, for food that afternoon, I ordered French fries with mayonnaise. These I always respond well to, and I like the combination.

Beverages, minus certain juices, are usually all right. Along with having more French fries for dinner, I had water, and a little later it was absinthe, served in a special glass. It tasted similar to liquorish. I thought of Ernest Hemingway, early on, and also his time in Cuba. He wrote about Pernod and seemed to like the beverage; I thought that it was very strong.

Then I went around the neighborhood, down streets, into places. Faces, all smiling back. It was really my first night out on the road, and almost all year for that matter, in this sense; I had hardly gone out to restaurants, bars or other venues at night after the pandemic began, because of the restrictions, but that night marked the end of them for me, essentially, and the start of this—the big event, and a lot of pain, another ordeal.

3

At one point I was walking around with a local kid, and the next moment I was in the back seat of a car with a girl and her friend, who was driving. We were moving very slowly, it seemed, through the streets. We went around with the windows up, and in the back seat I sat like a hostage, semiconscious. Then, after pulling over to the curb and for some reason getting out of the car, I stood there quite daunted watching the taillights slowly moving away, then turning the corner, and people filling the space. People, all journeying, to the end of the night.

On the walk again, seeing faces, seemingly different. I checked my wallet; my debit card was gone.

I remembered, what to do, what to do... I thought of The Honda, then walked back to Ursuline Street and got inside the car and pressed the start button. Not even the power turned on. I went to the front door of the hotel, the only door, and it was locked.

At check-in, I remembered, the clerk had said, "There will be no one here at the desk after 11pm, until 7am. The front door locks and you'll need your room key to get inside."

But I reached into my pockets and my room key was gone.

I thought of Hemingway again, thought what would he do? I considered getting food, realizing that it might be a long night. I was there, but it could have been anywhere. I was somewhere, and then I was walking somewhere, thinking, was I watching my drink and even my food. Then at once I was back inside The Honda, but I was hardly even aware of where I was, and after being unable to recline the seat because the car was full with storage bins, I woke up on the sidewalk.

That I remember, and I also remember walking through the neighborhood, up and down the streets, as the sun was rising, and so was the temperature. But I did not remember why I was walking; then, that the hotel door was still locked, that's why. Locked as of... whatever time it was or had been then, but it must be open now. And then—looking around, wondering—but where is it? And—everything seemingly the same—where am I?

4

It was very bright. I had to squint. Buildings wrapped around the streets, or the streets wrapped around the buildings. The neighborhood blocks went on and on. I was at an intersection, then reached for my cell phone, the first time that I had done so that day, and my phone was gone.

That I also remember, and I remember sometime during the night I was holding my phone, a phone, but at that moment I did not have it, any phone. So, I had a very hard time finding my way back to the... hotel. But, what was the name of it? And the street that it was on, the name of that, was...

"It starts with a V," I said to a police officer stopped at a stop sign.

"No street starts with a V around here," he said. Then he slowly drove away.

I asked a few passersby for directions. But when where you're trying to go to is unknown at the moment, directions are very hard to get. Then I asked for a map... "Just to see where we are right now, because I have a good idea of where *it* is..."

And that would be the hotel, the street, The Honda, or really, anything. Or really, everything...

The streets then cleared, and I stood alone, dazed. I walked, walked. I saw the city rising and the sun rising with it. Every day it does, clouds or no clouds. I walked around thinking, and not the first time thinking, my god, what happened...

A girl was running on the sidewalk toward the sun. She turned the corner at the intersection, and then I turned the corner at the intersection—first starting to vex, then smiled. People were beginning to step outside again, and they smiled. We were all on Ursuline Street—Ursuline, starting with a U. And I stood, not alone anymore, but before The Honda, facing the hotel. Feeling some ephemeral relief, I patted the car's bumper, then approached the hotel. The door was open, and there all the problems awaited a solution, or perhaps, a good outcome, recognition. So, I went inside.

Chapter 2

The clerk came over to the table with another cup of coffee. He then sat down behind the counter, as I talked and talked on the hotel's phone. It later became very very upsetting, damaging, having to deal with everything, these problems, on top of many other problems, and somehow the sun kept rising. The first problem that I thought of, as seriously as the others, was the car…

The tow truck would arrive in one hour, that's what I was told, so I had some time to solve another problem. Or at least, I thought, try to solve another problem. However, when one problem virtually rolls into another problem, not causing an additional problem but adding to the problem and having almost a snowball effect, there seems to be no end of problems. That is, until the ball stops.

Luckily, I had my laptop. The clerk saw that I was on it, the good old MacBook, which had been safely inside my room all night, and the clerk suggested using one of the apps that might have been on it to find my phone. So, I looked up the support number for Apple, and using the hotel's phone, I called them next because being unrested and stressed—I needed someone to help me through the process. Then, after waiting on hold for some time, right away I encountered another problem. I was locked out of The Cloud, and without my phone, I could not receive a verification code sent to my phone to reset the password. And just then, just then at that moment, I received a momentous email. The find my phone app had been disabled; from my cell phone. Not me? Sign into The Cloud to reverse this action…

"Well," a representative from Apple said. "That means someone has your phone and they got into it. And since you can't sign into iCloud…"

"Yeah?"

"I would deactivate your phone."

"Okay."

After that, I looked up the number for Spectrum. I called them to deactivate my cell phone, because only service providers are able to, but I could not get verified. Next, I called one of the few phone numbers that I remembered, for advice. It was don't deactivate your cell phone, could turn up. But I thought that I should, right? I took a sip of coffee, deep breath. Then, as soon as I had a moment to think of *what to do*, the tow truck arrived and I had to put this problem on hold—to attend another problem.

I left everything that I had with the clerk behind the counter, then went outside. Oh, how the day had changed. It was pouring rain, big, heavy raindrops. There were puddles everywhere and streams in the street. The tow truck pulled over. I was standing on the sidewalk, in the pouring rain, cold, discouraged, and drained.

"Can I get a ride to the dealership?" I yelled.

The raindrops were loud. They had an effect that was like white noise, muting even the strongest voice, and I had to try again. He rolled down his window and said, "Waiting on you!"

I got in the truck on the passenger side, then he got out. He had to get the car onto the back of the tow truck, somehow, by himself. I meant to offer help. Then I looked in the mirror and it was already there. He opened the door, got inside.

"That engine," he said. "Sounds like some bad gas."

But I did not wonder, since the car would not turn on, how the engine could have even made a sound. Feeling so strange, I thought that it was almost funny at first—if it was only bad gas. But it was not funny—there were all the other problems on hold, like a phone call…

We drove to the Honda dealership. My car went into the garage. I waited and waited for a while, sitting on a small couch inside a reception area. I still had my credit card, but my debit card was gone. I still had my will—or rather my strength of will—but no device or internet. What is Apple's number, Bank of America's, etc.? Almost all my things seemed to be gone, and all that I had, besides a card, was *my*self. Then, I realized another problem: I had to call my landlord because I was supposed to be moving into a new apartment the following day, and I had to call them to let them know that I might be a day late—depending on the car troubles and the other problems, if there is a good solution, or if there is a far-reaching outcome.

I asked the Honda receptionist to look up my landlord's phone number, and the receptionist seemed annoyed, oblivious to the problems, but I got it. Then I tried a phone in the waiting room, dialed the number and called the landlord. I mentioned the problems that had arisen, and I was told that I still have to pay the security deposit and first month's rent by the end of the day or I won't be able to move in. But I was at the dealership, and like I said, I had no device, no internet, no way to make the payment. The situation, or at least how I saw it then, appeared more clearly—I have to wait for my car to come out of the garage, and as soon as it does, as long as it is fixed, I will have to go back to the hotel and hope that my laptop is still there, safe with the clerk behind the counter, and then make the rental payment by 5:00pm—as long as no other problems arise. But there were all the other problems on hold as well, and the receptionist, for some reason, was unwilling to look up anymore numbers, at that point, for customer support, or anything else. So, on top of those problems, and that situation, there was a time factor as well. It was 1:00pm. I had four hours.

Just before 2:00pm the car came out of the garage. The service manager said that it was ready to go, and that driving it should now be good. I pressed the start button and it turned on; everything was on. Then I left the dealership and stopped

8

at the store to get a Tracfone, and the same issue occurred again. I hit the button and the engine shut off, but the power stayed on.

I still got the Tracfone, an inexpensive, basic flip phone, then went back to the dealership. My car went into the garage, again. And I waited and waited on a couch in the reception area, again, without internet, unable to make the important phone calls, and the rental payment, as I watched the clock approach 2:30pm, 3:00pm, then 3:30pm. Then, at almost 4:00pm, The Honda came out of the garage. The service manager said that this time they replaced the battery, and that now, he assured me, it should work. I mentioned the possible bad gas. And he said, "No, it was just the battery."

Okay... I thought.

This time, I tried starting and stopping the car before leaving the dealership. The Honda turned on completely, and then it turned off completely, the engine, power, everything. It seemed to be working properly again. So, I left, and somehow I found my way back to the French Quarter, back to Ursuline Street, and then back to the same spot in which The Honda was parked the day before, right in front of the hotel, the Villa Convento.

I went inside and then into the lobby. My bag, my laptop, my clothes, and everything else that I had were still there, safe with the clerk behind the counter. He could tell that on top of the long night, for me it had been a long day.

I poured a cup of hot coffee, sat at the table, and opened my laptop. I had a sip. It was good.

The clerk said, "Do whatever you need to do. You're welcome to stay as long as you'd like."

It was 4:30pm. Luckily I made the payment to the landlord on time. It was an online payment. My checking account was already linked to the portal, and I saw that the payment went through. I received a conformation email. Then two minutes later, literally, two minutes later, I received the first, *very*, troubling email. It was from Coinbase, a financial exchange app on my cell phone, and it was also a confirmation email.

Then I received another conformation email, from Coinbase, almost immediately, and then another, and another, and more. Not one email, or two emails, or three emails, but several; I did not know how many there were. They said something close to, "Thank you for your transaction. Your funds have been successfully withdrawn." Then, "Your funds have been successfully transferred." And then, "Your funds have been successfully sent." There were several emails, many even, and they were all closely related. Each one had a dollar amount, three thousand, four thousand, five thousand, plus…

Seeing that money just disappear, my heart drummed like the sound of the night.

The next hour was somewhat of a blur. I believe that I first called Bank of America, and because I was calling from an unrecognized phone number, I had to get verified. And the only way to get verified, to get access to my account, to even see my account, was by having a code sent to my phone. Only, it had to be sent to the phone number on my account…

"But I don't have my phone," I said. "Someone else has it."

"Well. They might get into your account."

"But they've already emptied it."

"Well…"

After the phone call I poured more coffee. The clerk started whistling softly. He seemed very sympathetic toward the issue. No words could express how either of us felt.

I gathered the rest of my things and then went to my room. I set down my bag and my laptop, washed my face, and then it happened. The nightmare, which was actually a realization, occurred. My notes were gone. All of my notes written on my phone were just gone. Locked out of The Cloud, there was no way to retrieve them.

They, them, me, and my are all different. But, I thought, it seems like "my" is no longer mine…

Then, after sitting down at the table—being locked out of everything but my room, my car, and my laptop—I started on another line, with another idea, a response, to all that I had made.

I wrote, "Oh, no. Not my notes! Just taking my notes, or rather stealing my notes, don't do that! Recorded thoughts, ideas, and associations; these notes are all basically a kind of currency. It's not necessarily money that will make the world go around; it's noted thoughts and ideas that will help the world and direct humanity."

The latter part of that thought is what some of the notes showed. But I only had the time and energy for one thought, one note—that night. There were calls to make, more problems to solve, and I was exhausted. After writing it down and tending to all the problems for a while, I went to bed. And in bed that's what I thought about, my notes, ideas, and some experiences.

Chapter 3

How they were written was simple. Each experience was memorable, and that is why writing about them, without them, the notes, should be easy. From hiking to camping, walking to running, swimming to driving to even just exercising, they ranged far and wide. And they were good. Like, "Hold on…"

"I will tomorrow. Nothing makes sense to me right now. But it will…"

I started recording notes to be a better writer, and I enjoyed writing them, as foundation for the next book. I thought that they were good enough, or at least that the book would be good enough, to win a Pulitzer Prize. And that made me happy. They consisted of many experiences which in a way were intended to fuel the book, not only form the book, and I knew that there would have to be even more experiences for the next book. Just realizing that, what they might be, what it could be, excited me. It made me happy. I had a desire to try and help the world, save the world and just help it, and that also made me happy. I still do, and somehow, I still am.

That leads to the question, what is happiness? It varies per person, but there are some similarities, qualities that everyone shares, things that everyone feels at some time or other, that makes everyone happy.

When there's less, there's more. And when there's more, there's less.

So, I'm in a bit of a bind with happiness.

Like, happy, happy happy.

However, looking at the meaning of bind... I would really like it, and feel very happy, if I had the privilege to be the apprentice, of, the chief.

That was just an example of the notes, what they were like. I had recorded about a book's worth of them, so there were many ideas, thoughts, pages, and altogether, they were of great worth. I wrote the first three or even five books without recording really any notes. I sat down at the MacBook and worked in the moment. But, recording notes in the moment... Doing that, I thought, might earn a trip to New York City, if not Washington D.C. Big things, definitely, happen in the moment.

The original notes, before they were suddenly taken, started on a camping trip just after I had finished writing *Any Moment*. The notetaking really started in the middle of it, not on the first day there, but on the following day, hiking through the Ventana Wilderness. There, the campsite, was along a ridge in the Big Sur area of California.

That morning, I made a few faces, got a few looks. Then at breakfast, I thought, aye! There's something in my eye and eye can't see. Luckily eye have three...

And I can see—that, that, and that person are all entirely different worlds. One world cannot be compared to another world, but only experienced. So, don't compare that world to mine. I have a whole explanation for why, and it's just impossible to do...

Then, after ending that thought, that note, and for a moment closing my eye, I set off, off, off on an adventure...

I drove forty miles along the Pacific Coast Highway and then arrived at the Big Sur Station. I parked in the lot, packed my bag, then went on a hike where the real notetaking began.

On the way there I had thought, what a mystical place! There was all this fog along the coast, and even just a short distance away there was very little that could be seen. It was almost disappointing. In Los Angeles, where I had been living, it was sunny and warm. In Big Sur it was sixty degrees and the sun was behind all the fog. Along the coast and even up the ridge at the campsite there was condensation in the air, everywhere. I kept going as though I was driving in a storm, the fog was so dense; for all I know, it could have been through a cloud. Then, five or ten miles down the road, there was either an arch, a tunnel, or a monument that was built going through the edge of a ridge, a prominent rock formation where the land met the ocean, and driving through it, or more so approaching it, was amazing. At some point further along the highway, tucked under some trees and behind a fence, was the Henry Miller Library. I kept going along the highway, and there was still fog, but somehow it seemed bright, felt light. Well, I thought, it should be a good day for hiking…

It was chilly at first, after getting out of the car, so I put on a rain jacket. Then from the parking lot I went along a short trail and ended up in the middle of a campground. This is an important detail because the actual trailhead started in the campground, but from the trailhead and also inside the campground, that short trail leading back to the parking lot, where my car was parked, was hidden and very hard to see— even in the daylight.

It was where where was, for a moment, not where I could see, and I made no note of it then, the notes started along the trail. The trail was pristine, and naturally the notes started right away.

It was simple as hiking along the trail. Easy to follow, as a good idea. But sometimes the best trails and the best ideas are more, intricate.

The trail there was very interesting. It gave me some great ideas and inspired notetaking. The entire hike I did not stop to take a rest, only to take notes, except at the "hot springs." But the hike there was worth it, as long as it was.

I got off to a later start than I had hoped for, sometime around 7:00am. I had breakfast at a café, unplanned. My stomach felt slightly upset afterward. It was something that I ate, one of the foods that I should not consume. Quality of life was only somewhat affected, and then after driving for an hour, everything returned to normal. It was around 10:00am or 10:30am when I started on the trail. Getting to the hot springs was a long hike into the wilderness. About a mile or two in, the fog cleared, at least where I was. The sun was out and strong along the ridge and further inland, and above this area the sky was blue. But, as soon as the trail wrapped around the ridge and changed direction and gained elevation, and the whole view from the ridge to the mountains to the ocean opened up, I saw that a great blanket of fog was still covering the coastline, and it was spectacular. Just a few miles apart the climate was completely different. There it was, wet. And at this point, here, the trail was exposed and the sun was strong but not too hot. Many lizards crawled across the path as I walked by; as I breathed in through the mind.

I went up and down mountains, along ridges, through meadows, and almost, it seemed, through the blue sky. There were big trees, fresh, green leaves, butterflies, dragonflies everywhere. The smell and the brightness were rich, great. I felt pretty good. And to think, I never thought that I would ever be there, anywhere, feeling much.

Then I really started feeling it, basically with every step, as the trail went up and down, toward the mountains and beside the valley. It was steep too, and there were just as many long stretches of going up as there were of going down. Some parts of the trail had big trees on either side, but still, there was very little shade. Many long stretches going up or down a ridge were almost bare on either side, and here there was no shade at all, just sun. I did not know the difference, between hiking up the ridge and the entire time looking at the top, or watching forty-five minutes the entire time go by on a clock. Looking in the eye of the sun. But more so, it was either going up or going down. Going up was strenuous on the legs; going down was hard on the shoulders and the feet. Either way it took about the same time, and maybe about the same effort, but not quite.

It was not until at least a few miles along the trail that I stopped for water. I looked out. Across the valley were a couple of mountain peaks. The trail seemed to be heading in that direction. And along the trail, on either side and down the valley, were more just massive trees. Big, charred trees. Their whole outer layer of bark was completely burned. But it seemed like they were still thriving, towering over all the others, taking in the sun. They had probably survived multiple wildfires over hundreds of years. That's how many rings they had, hundreds, and they were still standing. The strong ones were, at least, and that is incredible—no. Willpower is incredible—yes. Seeing it up close like that was incredible, that big tree, just as an inherent part of nature. Incredible that the tree is alive, still standing, and to be, interesting.

Ah, nice day, nice day. The trail sort of went past those two mountain peaks; it changed direction and followed the Big Sur River through a valley and offered much more shade. I had my little vaporizer pen with me; I thought, this is phenomenal.

Some rocks were placed as a bridge or a crossing from one side of the river to the other. I walked along them, carefully, to the other side. Then the trail went up the ridge, further and further into the wilderness. The final two miles of the trail, to the campground, were hard.

But I made it to the hot springs, at last. It was just after 3:00pm when I arrived. Then I undressed, had a nice swim. I sat on a big rock on the bank and dried off naturally. It seemed like all I could think about after when was where, where, but at that moment, this was where. And it made a few good notes.

Suddenly there was a splash, and then a divine voice, some laughter. I turned around. Two girls were in the water upriver. I noticed all their gear. They were probably camping nearby that night. It was a good spot—the campground, river, hot springs. No one else was there. No clouds were in the sky, just sun, tall trees, ferns, plants, grass, and the wonderful sound of flowing water, birds calling. We were deep in the

Ventana Wilderness. I thought, I'm just going to stay sitting on this rock on the bank of this river. Yes, that's all—eating kiwi, drinking water, having some, huckleberries. This is good, yes. Life right now is good.

The girls came up to me, asked if I knew where the hot springs were. But I thought that the river was the hot springs, and at first, they thought so too. The water was refreshing and clean. Then they went off looking for the hot springs. I stayed on the riverbank, and then a little later I found the trail and went on my way. I wondered if they had found the springs.

Downhill going back was the easiest. But it was not easy—at all. I know that I meant to take some notes on the way back but really it was getting late and the sun was growing dimmer and dimmer and though it was still light at that time I did not care to stop and write so I went fast along the trail and at the very end of it, going through the campground, I got lost. It took time to find the parking lot. Then I forgot what I meant to write. So I wrote this instead.

I did not get back to my campsite until 10:30pm. It was intense driving up the dirt road in the dark. There was a lot of skidding. And there was traction. But not as much going uphill. I was thinking, thinking I had something to say, but what was it?

Then, at the campsite, I thought of something else. Under the stars I seemed to be very in tune with the universe, and the thoughts just came to me, about what could and should be performed, for humanity. Like, setting a goal, and everyone working toward that goal, instead of many different entities competing against each other, working not necessarily toward something, but almost, in a way, working toward chaos. Kind of like every entity for itself. Of course there are some exceptions. But with globalization, instead of a near fractal-like free-for-all, maybe it could and should be all for each other. But what the goal actually is, or the direction, well, that's some food for thought. Only a kind of ambassador could figure that out.

Only he or she would wonder, "How do you know we're not just continuing an existence, this creation, from galaxy X, or Y?" "Their" existence happened in their world on their planet or some other kind of medium, and maybe we're just continuing that existence, their creation, over here on "our" planet, Earth. And it will continue, maybe here or maybe somewhere else. But while it's here, this thing called creation, why not try to make it last? In any event, that is how a goal will help. It just takes some time to think of one.

Chapter 4

After hiking for at least ten hours, that night I slept... all right. In the morning I rinsed off with water, then sat and looked out at the Pacific. Again, it was all fog along the coastline. But this time, further out beyond the fog was blue water and then a light horizon and blue sky above. I stayed in the chair and read for a little while.

Later I drove down the ridge and on the highway. I went past the Henry Miller Library, then the Big Sur Station, then turned around and went down a narrow canyon road toward the beach, but not just any beach, Pfeiffer Beach! No wonder there was a long line of cars at the entrance, but they were not in front of me. A few cars drove down the road behind me, and then several more arrived while I was waiting at the entrance, one of at least a dozen cars lined up and I was the last one let in. It was great. It somehow felt inspiring, like some good luck.

My first thought at the beach was... Well, I could not believe what I was seeing, mountainous bedrock formations right in front of the beach, huge waves crashing onto the beach, onto the bedrock, all the foam, blue sea, blue sky, altogether. I thought, a person who is color blind sees this place differently than I do. But it's not the place or even the world that's different, it's the mind, and every mind is different.

Then I walked around a bend to the right and laid down a towel. My spot was further back on the beach toward the base of the canyon, Sycamore Canyon, and its steep uneven walls. It was very windy, but all sun and maybe paradise, or at least, a paradise.

I thought that my spot next to the canyon walls would block the wind, but these winds were coming from the Pacific, full tilt, right at the beach. There were some marvelous waves. But the wind! I turned over onto my stomach. And my stomach felt good. I felt good. I opened a miniature bottle of champagne and then started reading. I went back and forth between the two. Had a sip, flipped the page. Ah, very nice, very nice.

At one point, I learned that Point Loma was the first place that European settlers landed on what is now the California coast. I thought that that was interesting. Then, I thought it was interesting that I have been there, that I have felt what maybe they had felt. But I have not even been to Europe, just everywhere, so I have not really felt what they were feeling...

Meanwhile there were many seabirds sitting right next to me, and I felt even more relaxed, good. But the wind, was, distracting. I was reading at that moment, but only reading the words, not seeing the words, studying the book. And that's not good, that's a problem. I set the book down, looked out. I thought, I know where I am; but wondered, where am I? Then, facetiously, where was I last night when I got lost?

There was a lodge and a patio and a staircase and maybe rooms to a hotel and I walked through the night on the Pacific Coast Highway and had no reception, no service, but still found the Big Sur Station. That alone added some leg to the hike, and I surely felt it.

That afternoon I got back to the campsite early. A few locals maybe drove up the road in a truck. One said, "This was my spot!" Then they drove on up the ridge.

It was a nice spot.

And it was free. I thought, maybe, when the most essential elements and compounds supporting life are free, why do some elements and compounds cost money? Imagine if someone owned the sunset. It was so spectacular that afternoon it seemed tangible. The fog spread out over the ocean and appeared as dense as clouds, and the sky was orange, yellow, pink, red, mixed with blue. Green was not part of that picture.

Chapter 5

After watching the sun go down, I went to bed, then woke up early, rinsed off with water, ate some grapes. I set off on the dirt road down the ridge at 8:00am. It was so foggy that water droplets formed on the windshield. Neutral gear was convenient; The Honda was working properly. I stopped at the café for coffee, ate a light breakfast, eggs. It was my father's birthday and I asked about Wi-Fi, to send a text message, but there was none. The proprietor told me about a hot spot along the highway where he would usually get reception. So, that's where I went afterward.

I pulled over to the side of the road and sent a text message. I thought that he would probably like Big Sur, that many would, its beauty, mystery, purity, it's perfect, this one-of-a-kind place in the seaside wilderness. And, I should mention, its remoteness. There were people around, but not many. I wondered what would happen if your car broke down out there. Besides this little hot spot on the side of the road, there was no service for fifty miles in either direction. But at least my car was running smoothly—at that moment.

I drove further down the road and then stopped at the Henry Miller Library. I picked out a book and talked with the shopkeeper. He saw my last name spelled out. I wrote it down, I believe, after we talked about books and the one that I had just written, my third book. I was amazed, he knew how to pronounce my last name. He said "Terrio" as though we were in France, or Canada, or…

"You're the first person in a while to say it right."

He said, "I lived on the island of Tahiti for twenty years. French is the official language. I'm from Sweden; I had to learn it. There—I had to learn it there. Just talking. Talking, then speaking myself. Are you French?"

"Part, and part Italian. But I was born in America."

"How long are you in Big Sur?"

"Indefinitely." I laughed. "I'm camping along a ridge in Plaskett. It's my little reward for writing the book."

"You know, I heard that everyone has at least one book in them. But three in one year. Yeah," he said. "You deserve a reward."

"Well. The latest one is good. It might be my best book yet."

"I'll read it." He looked outside and said, "See them setting everything up out front? All those tents and tables. My man is having his daughter's birthday party here this afternoon at 4:30."

"Oh, it's my father's birthday too."

"Really? It's her fifteenth birthday. Big celebration."

"The quinceañera?"

"Yes! Come back later if you'd like, you're welcome to."

"Oh, I might. I'm going hiking so if I still have some energy I will."

"Enjoy it, man." He smiled.

I got my book—*Island*—and then went to Andrew Molera State Park. It was about ten miles down the road, and it already seemed exceptional, just because it was Andrew's park.

I went through meadows, forests, hollow trunks of giant redwoods, I believe. I crossed a river several times, had to go back. I saw a deer prance across to the other side. It was a great warm up. The fog cleared by the time that I made it back to the other trail, and then I crossed the river again, the Big Sur River, and followed the trail down by the sea to a gorgeous intersection. Every direction was beautiful, pleasing. I went up a ridge along a partially paved road, up and up and up, I could not look back, yet I did, and I reflected, that it is hard to do.

Going along this carriage trail, I could almost see people at one time navigating this road on horse-drawn carriages. I could almost see French authorities, government officials, generals, going up the ridge on a horse-drawn carriage to Henry Miller's cottage. Then, after arriving, awarding him a medal, giving thanks for his depictions of Paris, its lasting significance, and what his literary work, though possibly controversial, had accomplished. Wine was poured, tears shed. "Well, Henry," they said. "This is paradise."

"Tchin-tchin." "Santé." "Santé."

Yes, I thought. And then I saw the paradise myself, I always had, it was always there. Birds chirping, singing, blue sky, sunlight, above coastal bluffs, along ridges, through meadows, trees, green vegetation; no wonder people from all around the world call this place where land meets sea paradise. There are different types of paradises around the world, and that is one of them. I'd like all of them.

In any event, along the trail atop the bluffs I definitely was, free of discomfort.

It was windy, it felt a bit chilly, put on a jacket, perfect. It was inspiration point, buena vista, looking out at the sea as though the world were infinite. That far up, that far out—woah. The joy will really make you, almost, cry.

I got back to the parking lot, still the afternoon. I had talked to a couple at one point along the trail on the bluffs. They asked if the trail looped around and went up the ridge, and it did. But they were back at the parking lot then, and they were looking at me, as though checking something out. And, I'd like to.

I had a good snack, fresh fruit and peanut butter, foods that I can enjoy and still really enjoy everything else. I noticed that there were many cars and people in the parking lot. However, other than myself and the couple, there were only a few people hiking through the park along the ridge and then the bluffs. As for the cars, I noted, not as many muscle cars as Los Angeles, but more trucks. I finished my snack, then left the state park and went south. I drove past the Henry

Miller Library. It was 7:30pm. They were still having the quinceañera, and it was a perfect afternoon. There were cars lined up down the street. And loud music. It sounded like a good time. Salud, I thought. But I did not stop. I enjoyed the hike. I was just trying to get back and read the book that I had bought earlier. Then I raced along the Pacific Coast Highway, at sunset, passing through the meridian of time.

Chapter 6

In the morning I made my first, small, one-log campfire in Big Sur. Five minutes later I got caught. I packed my things, cleaned up the spot, then drove down the ridge. It was about time to leave the camp. My own bed, getting restful sleep, seemed too sweet. Three days later I still thought that it was definitely a good trip. I was glad that I did it, and I would go back if I ever got the opportunity again. I never thought, even two or three months before the trip, that I would ever make it to Big Sur, let alone stay there for four nights camping along a ridge on a random dirt road uphill a couple of miles. And seriously uphill. The car was worked, which was probably good. The Honda had gotten used to the stop and go traffic, and it did well in Big Sur. Then I slept very well after getting home from The Sur.

This I reflected while eating takoyaki—I'm still unsure if this is one of the foods that I can tolerate. They're a Japanese food, wheat-based, and I like them. It's the wheat that can be problematic. At that time, I was mindful of what I ate, and what I liked did not necessarily have to taste good, but more so feel good, internally.

Over the following few days, I tried to see the parts of Los Angeles that I had been trying to see and understand but had been too busy; or places were closed because of the pandemic; or there might have been some other reason, something else, that kept me inside. But the city might too big to experience all of it, in a whole lifetime, or for some, even understand it. Every time that I thought I understood the city, I saw something, some neighborhood, intersection, street, building, park, person, food, event, and so on, that I did not understand, and my comprehension of what is went off course.

Just driving on any thoroughfare or freeway in Los Angeles was almost a competition. Maybe that person who just cut someone off and then passed the next car in the bike lane was on their way to a wedding, or a graduation, or even parturition. There were multiple instances too, and they were all eye-opening. I always drove alert, going the speed limit or maybe a little over, if possible, but carefully. I departed, then arrived; or arrived, then departed. It's both, right? It was interesting though, seeing everything else along the way, especially the things that I did not understand.

Then finally I made it to the museums. I rode a trolley up a hill and got off at a beautifully built, perhaps concrete or marble or sandstone, estate.

When I tapped on the outside walls as though I was knocking on a door, it rang like the sound of tin, not concrete or marble or sandstone. I put my ear up to the walls and knocked. I did not understand, that a little detail, could be so, interesting.

First I walked through a courtyard. There were many visitors posing, taking pictures, and maybe just as many statues also posing, but in Renaissance, Roman, or Greek fashion. Even modern. I went inside one of the buildings. There were displays in every room and outside were gardens. Art was everywhere—china, vases, drawings, sculptures, photographs, manuscripts, paintings…

I saw a lot, and from what I saw, they said, "If I had never understood a thing that was illustrated in this painting, if after the time following creation there are only one idea preserved, *creative currency*, that is quite enough."

And that was all to see. I took the trolley down the hill. Then I drove on the freeway to the valley, going 70mph in the middle lane, watching some cars to the right driving ever so slowly, and some cars to the left driving fast. Then I got off the freeway and went through one neighborhood, then another, and another, and then I went up a mountain pass to my place on the boulevard—in Hollywood.

Chapter 7

Not long before this, someone had suggested going to Magic Mountain. It might've been my neighbor. She was trying to go at that time, but now she was away, somewhere. However, I still went. The morning of was exciting. But it was not until I was at the intersection, turning left into the entrance, that I realized or recalled how crowded amusement parks are. It seemed like everyone was trying to turn left. There was a long line of cars in the left lane. I could not gauge how far back the line went, but it probably went far. The problem was that cars in the middle lane were driving up to the intersection, then putting their blinker on and trying to get into the left lane, last minute. This caused an awful traffic jam—even in the middle of the intersection, at the crossroad. Lights turned green but no one could move. Somehow it still seemed like a competition. I just wanted an adventure; also, a snack, something to drink, eat.

Then I learned that it was not so easy. The line for the first roller coaster lasted well over an hour. Some mothers started talking to me. They were very affectionate toward their kids. One said, "We're just little girls inside big bodies."

I thought that was funny. There was a group of people in front of me, possibly college kids, and one said, "Na, USC's in the hood. UCLA has good parties. But, bro. Santa Barbara on 04/20..."

The line moved forward. One of the mothers asked me, "Why the amusement park instead of the water park?"

"I had a bad experience at a water park when I was younger. I got the flu. It was unpleasant. And, I like roller coasters."

"Great, we do too!"

She hugged and kissed her kid, then he pawed her chest.

"Are you people watching?"

"Not really. Just observing and meditating. I'm really zoning out. I've had an unusual past, few months. So it's nice to give my mind a little rest."

Further down, the line moved much faster. We went inside a building and stood at a gate. It was almost strange. There were many people yelling in the roller coaster station. It might have been anything. Like, "I want an adventure!" I thought, a beer, or something to eat. Then the gate opened.

"Have fun!" said the mother.

I got in the seat. I was toward the back of the roller coaster. Then we started moving. We left the station, and it was not until we were a little way up the lift when I realized that we were going backwards; I was quite zoned out. Then we dropped and how exciting. I forgot about the pleasure from being in free fall, that feeling of weightlessness. It was awesome. The roller coaster was fast, and I could not tell if we were going forwards backwards, or backwards forwards, or if we were upside down or right side up. Like living in the world, it was probably a combination of every which way.

We got back to the station. I walked out, then went around the park—in search of a place with good food and beverages. It was incredibly hard to find one, at least one without a long line, when it should have been easy to get both. So I went on more roller coasters. There was the one that started with a countdown and took off backwards from the station fast, then went straight up and for a moment I felt lighter than air and then went straight down back to the station. All the rides that I went on, but that one, had loops. And they all made my head rattle against the headrest and shoulder harness. I eventually got a headache, yet somehow, I remember, I still had some good ideas.

I mostly kept to myself for the rest of the day. One time this girl in line could not stand still. She was with a group, I think, and she kept talking, but maybe just to herself. I thought of my old friend, and then I thought of myself and him at amusement parks as kids, then of myself in line as a kid inside a big body, like the mother, and I remembered vaguely back then, I could be a motherlover. Maybe around four or five years old, the first amusement park experiences. There are traces of that kid, of course, parts of the past in memory. Then comes change in time, with circumstance, every event. So, a new perspective, a new skill, a new self and a new world develops. It was interesting though. It sounded like the girl was talking through her nose. It was adenoidal. I just thought that voices are unusual, and like names, one grows into their voice but not the other way around. And then, there are the lucky few who can change their voice on demand, and they might become the voice. But in that instance, the voice becomes them.

Toward the end of the day, after waiting in more lines, I finally got a beer. It was at a place toward the corner of the park, near an intersection of pathways, and I thought that it should have been free. The whole day was a test of patience, waiting, and even suffering. It was not only the beer that mattered, though I enjoyed it, it should have been free. After all that, it did not seem just to have to pay for anything. It had been a long day.

Then, maybe an hour later, I went out to my car, left and got on the freeway, and then drove to Hollywood.

Chapter 8

There was still so much to see with only a few days before the road trip. I went on the Metro Rail. There was a station close to my apartment, right at Vine and Hollywood. I walked by the Capitol Records Building every time on my way there, and also the Taft Building. Had there not been a pandemic, I probably would have gone inside these landmarks for an artistic career. Instead, I wrote two books in a fairly short time, determined to establish a literary career. Now I had time, at least a little, so I went down by the sea.

I drove there, to Venice Beach, listening to music, loving the tremolo. I was relaxed. Some cars flew by, but there was generally a line of cars, not jammed up, and I made almost every green light. As soon as the road opened, I went a little faster, moving with the music. I found a good spot and parked seaside. Then I walked along the pathways beside the canals. On a little bridge, going from one isle to another, I looked down the waterway—tree tops sticking out into view, a few canoes, docks, dinghies, signs by the shrubbery. Then a man came down the canal on a paddleboard. He waved, I waved. I thought, I do like it here, and I smiled—if I had a boat or else one of those to maneuver through the canals.

After that, I crossed the street and went to the boardwalk and met up with a photographer. She had a dog with her, a Maltese. Along the boardwalk there was a small garden off to the side growing right out of the sand. It had some flowers and some succulents, maybe aloes and agaves. Then at some point beyond the garden the boardwalk kind of stopped. We were going south toward the water inlet, trying to make it to Del Rey, so we walked leisurely on the beach. Every now and then there were sections of pavement, and then breaks in between with sand, as though there had once been a boardwalk but then somehow it turned to sand.

Her dog was running all around. "Oh, she's so excited."

It was a beautiful setting. The properties out front were all somewhat posh, a few people walking on the sand toward the water, and another person walking their dog and then going down a street. We went around the corner and followed the inlet, and in the water were many grand boats, some going east and others going west. There were sailboats, even yachts, and more. They were immense, impressive. It was necessarily something to experience. Seeing this sight was sufficient. But being part of the sight, oh, my mind had some fun.

Next we went down a pathway following a lagoon. It connected the canals to the ocean, and that was the direction we were heading, toward the canals. We crossed over a bridge at one point and walked along the other side, following the path the entire time, then going on the sidewalk, and then on the street.

"I love this."

She went up to a street sign. Attached to it was another sign, diamond-shaped, and yellow. It said, "Peacock Crossing."

I had seen it or one like it before. I did not know where it was, and maybe it was that one, but I had never been on that street before. Was it a déjà vu? It happened all the time, going down streets, through neighborhoods, seeing places that I had never seen before but feeling like I had. That was when, when I thought that I understood things, I did not. Wait, what—oh, yes?

It was inspiring, and what's rare, also interesting.

A little way down the street she said, "Aw, she's getting hungry." Her dog was following. I don't know how far we had walked. We saw many sights. And I felt good, still inspired. So much so that later, that afternoon, I got on the subway and went to downtown. It was a much different setting there. I went to Olvera Street first. It was a quick walk

33

from end to end. It did not seem like Los Angeles, but if there is but one street preserving the origin of Los Angeles, that was it, the old adobe, the vendors, the trees, vines, lantern lights. I would have liked the street to go on further, just for a day, but it was only about the length of one block.

There was too much going on to take notes. I was not actively writing anything down at this time that day, just after morning. But to let the ideas, oh, blend together in a way, inside the mind, so that the big ones and the smaller ones mix, that combination creates the best ones. And then when it is time to write something down, these ones come first. But there is also another method to this, and that is to just write everything down.

Anyhow, I was only observing. I walked along Broadway from the 101 freeway to Olympic Boulevard. This stretch of road, the Historic Broadway Theatre District, seemed very well historical. It was as though the street was still set in the early twentieth century, and over time the buildings remained untouched, under the sun. The theatre signs almost spoke their own language and used their own calligraphy. I pictured it back then, in the early twentieth century, and the street and the sidewalks were crowded with people waiting for entertainment. And how it has evolved. A century before that the first adobe house was built, then a century later the first high-rise was built, and now it is this, the next century will constitute everything.

It was basically a turning point, what the idea evolved into, before writing it down. Plus, the rest of the day was hard to describe.

Chapter 9

A common theme for at least a few of the days at that time was walking. But the theme overall has evolved from our origins by nature, only curly, first as explorers or conquerors, scouring new or occupied land for even just a sense of adventure. Then at some point the land stopped, and though it had always been finite since the start of time, this urgent inherent sense that dates back before time expanded and enlarged.

It might seem flowery to introduce a simple walk at sunset like that. There were two of these walks actually, and they were on the last two days before this self instinctively sprung up, or the last two days before setting out on an adventure that led to the big event and then to the arousal of that self. All that, or this, is coming from that urgent inherent sense that was passed down from our earliest ancestors. These two walks were not just simple, they were spectacular. That's because at sunset it was a new kind of setting, and in that case, almost new land, but a different world.

I went to Griffith Park one day and Runyon Canyon the next. I had been to both parks before, but this time, early in the evening yet close to night, they seemed different. One was a mile down the road to the right, and the other was a mile and a little more down the road to the left. The latter was Griffith Park, and that's where I went first. I walked on Franklin Ave, first under the overpass and then past a bookstore with a catchy pig sign out front. Going by I always thought about it, and I even dropped off my resume there before starting *Any Moment*. Could you imagine, someone who writes books writing books at a bookstore? Nonsense, the shelves have to be filled somehow.

This part of the avenue going east from my apartment was pleasant. The other direction, going west from my apartment, was better in some parts, except for one intersection. Either way they were set at the base of the hills, but both had a fairly different setting.

Where I was, approaching Western, the sun was starting to go down behind me. The road was lined with tall trees, and the tops were all green and golden. I went around the corner up Western and then around the bend to a trail in the park. It was a hidden oasis during the day, but that time, almost night, it seemed prehistoric. I marveled at the flora, ferns and the likes. This part of the trail was brief, and then I went on another up to the observatory. There the sun went down. It was a good aloha to the city. And it was similar to the following night, but getting there was different.

About halfway to the park built around the canyon was a castle. It is full of magic, or it seemed so from the outside. I mean really it was the Magic Castle and it seemed magical from the outside. Then there was the Highland Gardens Hotel, and just walking by was inspiring, thinking about all the legends that had stayed there. Go right down La Brea and at the end of the street there is this one-block street and it is one of the most pleasant streets in the whole city, unassuming, undisclosed.

I was in the park after dark, and then I saw the sunset over the city, and I felt great. Then I realized that, I had seen many sights, I might have seen the city or had at least begun to, but I had not fully experienced it. This was an unusual moment, indulging that I do, with the resources. And then the sun set, twilight came, the lights shone. I walked back to the apartment. It was almost empty, except for my bed, some furniture, and a few tables of various dimensions. I had packed everything else into The Honda, or else by the gate. It was full, set for a road trip. But the road is, unpredictable. It has that turning point, it has that intersection, that crossroad, competition, it is that roller coaster, personifying creation, it has problems awaiting payments, premiums, it has canyons, parks, sights, sunsets, trails, flora, magic, it is inspiration, it has its own voice and its own ideas, different dimensions, it has everything, that inherent sense of adventure.

Chapter 10

I set off early in the morning. I had coffee first, then got on the freeway. I thought of some families, or mega, mighty families, in Europe and elsewhere, manning the machine. There was the U.S. Bank Tower glowing at sunrise. And further inland stood Mt. San Antonio. The whole area was mountainous, not only bright with desert sun, but the rising sun. It could be called the commencement of a new day, and then throughout the day, of conception, and after several days, inception.

I did not write down anything for at least a couple of hours. It was not until Joshua Tree National Park when I could easily pull over onto the side of the road and begin to understand the setting that the notetaking on the road commenced. I wish I still had those notes, but I do not. As far as I know they were simple. Just the sight of a Joshua tree up close inspired the first thought. Its leaves were palmlike but also sharp, though not as sharp as the thorns on a cactus, but close, and it stood eccentrically built with its limbs extending cleverly like a cactus, up toward the sun. This one tree seemed to be a combination of a cactus and a palm, rising from the land, seeking the warm glow of the sun.

The original note started with this thought, one tree. But I cannot remember where it led to, only that it was good. It seems like a thousand miles away, only it was more. Going through Joshua Tree was not part of the original itinerary, nor was New Orleans. They were on the same road the moment I set off that sunrise, only they were slightly off course from the original route but still seemed thoroughly different, worth it, worth spending the extra time getting to, and going through, this new land.

There was one road that went in and out of Joshua Tree, and there might have been a few other roads inside the park, but only one that went from one end of the park to the other, north to south. It was at least fifty miles long. There were not many people nearby. But there was a lot of land, mostly the same landscape, and likely multiple deserts. I was not worried about the car, being out there under the sun and among the heat haze, but just excited to be on the road trip.

Once the freeway came into view I went faster. I got on and stayed on—until Phoenix. I made it there by early afternoon and had something to eat. Only a few foods at that point I knew would not upset the rest of the day—talking about food at the store at least, or food from a restaurant. So I stopped at the store, and from the hot bar I filled a bowl with rice, chicken thighs, some leafy greens, and oil. It was good.

No one said how Phoenix feels. Time on the road is almost limitless. In the desert there it was 3:00pm. To get the most out of it, out of the afternoon, I had a couple of options. Where I went after eating food was to a park by a body of water. Going swimming was technically an option, but probably not allowed. People were on boats and paddleboards and other kinds of watersport equipment. To cool off you had to go inside. Yet I went to a botanical garden instead. I had been inside all day, in a car, on the road, and this was the desert, the Desert Botanical Garden. I learned all about the indigenous people of the area, then wondered how they did it. They made the most out of the land, cultivated what they could, passed down knowledge. There were information displays in front of the exhibits. Much about how it was for the indigenous people was found on these displays by their replicated shelters. I went inside to see, ducked around, felt myself. I thought of Big Sur, sleeping on the ground up the ridge. Four nights was hard, but I did it. They did the same thing, in the desert, for centuries. And at the same time, across the ocean, we people did it in palaces. Or else, in a different desert, in Pyramids. In the future, there just might be other kinds of structures, more options.

My room for the night was in a house close to downtown. Some of the notes compared Los Angeles to Phoenix. Briefly walking around, I thought that what one was now might have been similar to what the other was like earlier in history, and it's expanding, it's in a transitional phase. Now, this term "transitional phase" is important. It is very simple, exactly what transitional means—changing or moving from one state or self or condition to another. And phase—a distinguishable part in a course or development, or an aspect or part of a problem under consideration. Phoenix of course was in a transitional phase, growing, and expanding. Whereas I was on the cusp of entering this phase. In fact, that sunrise I had already entered it. Just being on the road was a distinguishable course itself. Almost every second the setting was changing, and soon enough, on the road, that self changed to another self, not that day or the next, or the one after, but maybe it had already happened.

I went inside a restaurant, sat on a stool. They had a baseball game playing on the tv. The place was busy, so of course the Diamondbacks were playing, possibly at home. A girl was working on a laptop next to me and I asked what she was working on

It was just, "A personal book about the past seven years of my sex life."

"So is that for, private, use?"

But private, or privacy, is less and less personal. This was just one example.

Then, getting back to the game. The Diamondbacks won that night. They played the Padres. And the game was actually in San Diego, not Phoenix. Several times I had been to Petco Park, home of the Padres, but only around the outside of it. L Street, I remember, and one time I even had a long phone call right next to the park, the bottom of 7th. That had happened nearly a year earlier, and before setting off on the road that morning, I planned on writing a short piece based on that whole year, between one road and another. And then that turned into this—just a different, unexpected, part to a book.

I went back to the house and I think that my room used to be the garage but it was great. It had almost all that you need in there. It was air conditioned, clean, newly renovated. I felt good, and I fell asleep easily.

Chapter 11

The next overnight stop on the itinerary was in El Paso. This stretch of road from Phoenix to Texas, going through southeast Arizona and then southwest New Mexico, made the walls in my car dance. I thought that I understood the road, just by seeing it; had done the road a year earlier, but a different route. Up until Tucson I listened to some soft music that sounded good in the morning. I sipped coffee, steered the wheel. Then this city sprung up at the foot of some mountains. From the freeway, in the early sun, it looked golden. And then I started listening to audiobooks, through New Mexico. One thought that I had was, if only I went through Santa Fe... I had sent one of my early books that is no longer in print to the institute there, addressed to one of my favorite writers. He was one of only a few people to which I sent a copy. And, I thought that I might have beneficial or at least unique ideas to add, and that I would probably work well with the people there. Santa Fe, or at least the institute; their work, practices, insights, seemed, esoteric.

But I drove along the southwestern portion of New Mexico. There was sparse vegetation, grass, shrubs, but the landscapes, the arid valleys, distant mountains, ranges, were beautiful. And then I crossed the Rio Grande and shortly after arrived in Texas. My car was running low on gas. I had gone the whole day without stopping. I filled up, got food, left, and looked out over the city from a ridge above the base of a mountain—in the United States. There, I could see Mexico. It was hard to distinguish one country from the other, from where I stood, there was no discernible border. Instead, it appeared to be all part of the same land. And this land went on and it eventually reached a coastline, an ocean separating this land from other land, but at the bottom of it, it's all connected.

El Paso was the first city that I visited in Texas and it was a good stay. I saw the first flash of lightning and heard the first peal of thunder in about a year. I sat outside on the porch for a moment because it had also been that long since hearing and really smelling a downpour, that petrichor, and it was nostalgic. Then I spent the afternoon downtown, some of it at a plaza, and ultimately, feeling content, I went back to my room for the night.

It was a short morning. I took a shower and then got back on the road. That self then was just excited, for that world, the land, the book, possibilities, all good things.

Some people that I had talked to said that driving through Texas was boring, for some reason, but I thought the opposite. I took note of the changing landscape, going from the flatland frontier, across plains, through valleys, seeing hills, plateaus, rivers, arroyos, running water, somewhere, the vegetation changed from desert and grassland to nearly forest with trees and plants—in six hours to San Antonio.

Along the way I finished an audiobook. It was by a great American writer, and he was on the road too, traveling across America. What was surprising, I heard the phrase "Thanksgiving Orgy" multiple times as though it was a big event. Maybe he was saying something else and that's what I heard because it's what I was thinking about, and I thought that it would be interesting. It seemed like a good way to celebrate the day, at least on the road.

When I was a kid I thought that grownups had them all the time, maybe not on holidays, but I still got jealous. Then again, when I was a kid, I never went on any, extended, road trips. Also, it was ironic that this holiday feast if that's what it was apparently happened in Texas, as my belly was making noises.

In San Antonio, I stayed in a big house just off the freeway. There were Roman statues and a hot tub out front, and inside were several other rooms and maybe guests, but it was quiet and I thought that I might have the house to myself. Yet after bringing my suitcase inside, I went down the street for a walk along the river, a distinctive river. It looped around the heart of downtown, but unlike most other urban rivers. I was on American land but had I suddenly awakened there on the sidewalk without a phone or a GPS or directions or any idea of what is, and at the same time feeling so dazed and violated, for all I know I could have been anywhere.

I looped around the river at least once, then went inside a restaurant for French fries. "With mayo, please." Either that request was odd, or I said it oddly.

"I've heard worse things," said the bartender.

I ate the French fries quietly, paid, then left.

After leaving San Antonio the car drove normally, as usual, to New Orleans. There was no reason to be concerned about the Honda. I had no preparation for all that happened overnight and the following days. But somehow I navigated through it, the wheres and whats. I felt a drumming inside that was greater than ever before. I was supremely alert. What was sleep? Ah, what a nightmare. That's how you wake up a different person, being. All those things happening was possibly not a first, but happening all at once in the same night made it much much worse, and subsequently, the aftermath made it a nightmare, with a lot of distress under the surface, significant. It had to stop, couldn't. It just went on, too far.

Chapter 12

Two days after leaving the Villa Convento, I somehow made it to my MB apartment with what I still had. Luckily, despite my loses on that afternoon two days earlier, the landlord still received my rental payment. Three minutes later and they would not have. But they did. So, I was able to move in.

For two days straight The Honda stayed on. Its engine, and its power, would not shut off. Both turned on in New Orleans, in the morning, but after that, neither the engine nor the power shut off for two days. The start stop button after that morning was just ineffective. I pressed the button again and again and nothing happened. Then I went to an auto parts store, after arriving at the last stop on the itinerary, and they said that they could shut the car off from under the hood, I believe, but there would be no guarantee that it would turn back on. So, it kept going, nonstop, for two days, all the way to the dealership and then into the garage.

I did not know what was more frightening, my phone being taken, knowing that someone was accessing it, receiving those emails, or the car not shutting off, this big machine going at least 70mph, malfunctioning... That was on the road there, and the night before arriving there, I hardly slept. I had been driving all day and I got a room at a cheap hotel. There were people walking around outside all night, and all night the car stayed on, its engine, its power, nothing would shut off, and it also would not lock because it would not shut off, so I stayed up all night to make sure that no one would steal it. And also, because of all the problems, I was just, worried.

Fortunately, it was still there in the morning. I set off on the road and then arrived early, but I did not have enough time to unload my things, what I still had, what cannot be taken from, or what is not on, a cell phone. I got the keys to my apartment, from the landlord, and then I went straight to the Honda dealership. Along the way I thought that I had met an interesting person, the landlord or one of the girls at the office, because we share the same birthday, same day, month, and year. Maybe, for all I know, we share the same meridiem, hour, and minute. I had never met a person like that who has experienced the same number of sunrises as I have, and I thought that it was interesting. For a moment, I felt all right.

Then, at the dealership, I had to wait again. I was exhausted. There were so many problems, and after a while I went to the apartment, I was so insecure. The Honda had to get worked on overnight because there was a very unusual problem with it, I found out later that afternoon, and it was also very alarming...

Essentially, the power control module had been tampered with, from the inside. Upon inspection, the technician found several "aftermarket" wires around the driver under-dash fuse box. Connected was some kind of device, and the reason the car stopped working properly, or actually why it would not stop running, was because these aftermarket parts that were apparently taped together started coming loose and probably caused malfunctions with the power control module. Hence, *the car would not shut off at all.* So to fix the car the technician had to extract the device, then rewire and reset the power control module. And the car's warranty, which was supposed to give me a peace of mind while moving long distance in case anything happened, did not cover the fix, or the restoration rather, because this device and these parts were aftermarket, and they were aftermarket because the car had been tampered with.

Altogether, combined with the bill from New Orleans, after the first part of the event fixing the car was expensive monetarily. But how can you gauge a monetary expense when many other problems, or damages, were induced because of it and the problem? And then there were all the other problems that happened the first part of the event in New Orleans, on the same night, and all of the problems that those other problems caused as well, mainly with financial institutions. These problems from that night, and the problems with the car, caused many serious problems, or damages, that are difficult to gauge the cost of having to endure them. It is hard to put a monetary value on time, distress, suffering, feeling, injury, insecurities. With all these problems occurring at once, on top of everything else in the second part of this book, I don't know anyone else who could've navigated through it but, I just had to be the one.

Chapter 13

In any case, after getting worked on overnight, The Honda was ready to go the following morning. I just had a hard time getting to the dealership. That's because I had just moved in and arriving a day late caused some, additional, problems. But really, it was mostly because I did not have my cell phone, and because the internet technician had been unable to reach me, to get inside and set things up, I had no internet. I was not home on the day of the appointment, I was still on the road, a day late. And, not having my cell phone on the road, I was unable to call and reschedule the appointment. I had a Tracfone, but I did not call them until after moving in. They were closed for the long weekend, it was July 4, so I had to wait four extra days just to get internet access. I couldn't go to a public place with free internet; so daunted, I barely felt alive at that point.

Meanwhile, all the other problems, with Bank of America, the fraud department, Coinbase, Cash App, Apple Cash, and Apple support, had to be put on hold. For four days I was unverifiable, because I had no internet or cell phone. I was unable to prove, just because someone had stolen my cell phone, that I was even me. The other person could have, I suppose, if they felt up for it. It was, as if being in two places at once, just one big awful mix-up.

On top of that, upon moving in, the apartment was not ready, after having extra time to get it ready. The main light fixture was just hanging from the ceiling, much lower than it should have been, and so troubled, I kept walking into it. But mainly, it was the oven that was missing an essential part, and the store that sold it was apparently closed for the long weekend, so I was really unable to cook for five days. Then, right after things started coming together, but only at the apartment, not with all the other problems... I somehow split my thumb open while finally cooking on the stove. It happened because of all the problems, because I was so stressed out and exhausted, thinking about the car, that night, the following days, thinking why can't things be good?

I had a bowl in my hands, a big ceramic bowl, one that was sort of decorative, it was a nice bowl, and it hit the edge of the counter as I was bringing it to the sink, fairly hard I guess, because instantly... There was a loud noise, some kind of crack or smash, which was almost exciting. Then there was blood, a big open wound going up my thumb, and a big piece of ceramic that I had to pull out. Then, a big, "Uh oh..."

So, I went to the hospital. I waited in the emergency room at Mount Sinai Medical Center for three hours. Then I saw a doctor, in a small medical room, quickly. I got a dozen stitches. And then sometime later I received a bill for about $3,000, for waiting in the emergency room and seeing a doctor just to get stitches. And then there was an even longer wait, because I was unable to really use that hand for two weeks, plus...

Chapter 14

I got a new cell phone. I no longer had to use a flip phone, that Tracfone from the road, and I also had to get a new number. I thought, at least the website is still up and running, and my email is on there. I can still receive those, and I can still check that. But, my hand... At least it was only my thumb. But, only...

Fortunately, I was still able to do some things. I was only in a transitional phase, I could still think, I could still write, and I did both—just some notes on a thread of a Sunday afternoon. The date was 07/18/2021, and these are just some thoughts for it all, mostly unrevised and all unprompted. Like...

"Maybe right now the notes will start again. It's hard to tell. I start one note and I have no idea where it will go. Right now it's almost out of, hope, and that can produce some good ideas. So, I don't know where this note will go. I really should start writing about important issues, but I also really like takoyaki, with a glass of Sapporo. How much beer will I have this afternoon on this beautiful day? Some, but so far only one, gulp. Keep them coming. Right now I'm too skinny, too thin, from all the unexpected problems—and all the insecurities catching up, and then those getting figured out. Ergo, bulk up. So, more beer. I've never been much of a beer buff. I only have some on occasions. And I know how to drink a beer. But I suppose this is a silver lining. This first note...

"Same little thread, like a fractal, see where it goes... Well, on to the second one. Why do I get so much attitude from others? Can't they see that I'm just doing what makes me happy, seemingly busy writing these notes. Maybe they think I'm emailing brokers, placing bets, making Hollywood films... Oh, well I have lived there, in the extraordinary city of Hollywood, California. For now I will do these things, these strange little notes on this same little thread, in MB...

"The takoyaki is better than most places in Little Tokyo. It's good... What are more profound things to write about? Yes, the takoyaki is very good...

"It is strange though, going out after all that almost forces me to write these notes. Not a silver lining, but more like a win win...

"Oh, no. I just realized that all the extra problems, the reason why I've gotten so thin, down to a hundred pounds, seven inches... they're adding up by the day, I need to eat, extra!

"When one does not eat enough, problems, especially those in the follicle department, even though they have gotten better, they get worse...

"Street corn? No, elote. That's what I'm about to order, maybe, though ordering it takes... But if I could do what makes me happy and make money, man, all the suffering described in past books, and especially all that's described in this book, would mean nothing. There's more, and more to it, but I would be happy. I am. Just not, like that would be...

"Enough about certain feelings that seem to always brush my mind, what are the issues?

"Feed me another, please...

"Nas knew. He said it: 'Inclusion is a hell of a drug.' And it is an issue, not for me, not for him, but for billions of people it is...

"Ah, the mediums, one of my favorite songs is playing, 'I'll be missing you.' Thank you, this is a great song, and that is a great song, and both are two of my favorites. It's hard for me to describe, but in a way, this was inspiration for *Any Moment*, that was inspiration for *The One*. In a way, it was almost one for the other. My dream is to help the world... and get credit for it...

"Then, the idea. Do you believe in reincarnation?

"I did not know that this is a chain restaurant, and I've possibly had one of these tacos before. I lived right next to one in Los Angeles, and now I live right next to one still, and there are many people here, and there. There are also locations in Boston, Houston, et cetera. A lot of locations to have a good, time…

"So, then why am I going somewhere else for food? Ah, because I'm too thin, because I'm down to about a hundred pounds, seven inches… These problems, they feed one off the other…

"Like her. And her. And huh. Three, pm…

"Maybe in Hollywood it seemed like I was an actor or otherwise had some role in the movie industry. Maybe I do, did, and I do not and did not even know it. Or I do, and more, just by making notes. People are always going to buy movies, it can be anything, I just think that I could probably help spruce or spice up the meanings of the movies that are made, just to help make them. Plus, right now, somehow I look all right, could be all right, and it would probably be a good idea to preserve that…

"I should get some calories soon… That could just be some food for thought, what I'm talking about. Still, it's a start, or a part…

"The tables I've been sitting at always seem to wobble…

"How come no one seems to want to help me find Adderall? The book will be hard enough as it is to write. Maybe it's all right. It is all right. I haven't had any in years, and it's not good for the stomach, especially… So much more would be thought of, completed…

"Happy, sad…

"There is a pile up of about five cars outside, and nothing seems to be getting done, no one is moving, they're all waiting, cars and cops and people standing all around. And no one would've guessed…

"I remember the expression on someone's face, in San Diego, after they were unexpectedly hit by another car of the freeway. It was a serious expression. I felt, and sometimes feel, probably what he was feeling, plus…

"In this little thread I reflected on one quote, one thing that Nas has written. And then there's all I've written, the under-surface pain…

"I'm wondering, why seem unhappy? Me, not everyone can pick between happiness and suffering. Maybe both are always there, present, compatible. But sometimes there can be enough of one to overpower, or rather mask, the other. Then, that state of mind becomes almost imperceptible. And when it's one or the other, it gets tricky. Maybe it will never be understood, or studied, what either really are…

"But I do understand one, more than the other. I know it too well…

"This is just a little thread of notes of an ordinary afternoon. Time to get back to this, right now, is making me happy…

"Anywhere, everywhere… The adventure awaits…

"Seeing all these people people watching, anywhere, everywhere, is interesting… When I'm the one being watched, what I understand, it might be hard to gauge. That is…

"Hmm…

"My finger, my thumb, is not healing. It's almost getting worse… Really, it is a bit concerning, it has no feeling, except for, hurt…

"I am not going to litter tonight, I never do. Seeing it happen upsets me. I'm just glad that I did not eat anything that upsets my belly, which causes some suffering…

"My thumb is definitely injured…

"Did all the problems in the world, the drastic problems, start arising when… When was it before, or was it after, or was there always, a transitional phase…

"But it's much more than that, it's my thumb, and it depends on…

"Care."

Before all the notetaking began again at last, recording those thoughts of a Sunday afternoon, I went back to the dealership and retrieved my car. It drove home so smoothly, almost as though it had been revived, and in a way, it had been. It, like me, was also in a transitional phase.

Ever since getting the car, it had been inside either a locked garage or a gated lot the entire time, and throughout that time the car itself was also locked. Yet it was still tampered with. Then, thinking of my locked cell phone, its six-digit passcode, my notes, and money, I gulped, carrying the whole weight of the world.

Part 2

The Insecurities

Chapter 15

I'm fairly certain that insecurities are innate, or in that case, almost inevitable. When I was born, by caesarean delivery, there was already an imbalance of internal microbiota. That itself might have caused some of the complications; although unlikely, maybe asthma. Luckily that condition corrected itself early on, but others continued, for a very long time.

It all started with the yellow toenail. This dates back to the earliest memories of childhood. From then on, throughout the early years, I had one toenail that was yellow. It was on my middle toe, left foot, and I was very insecure because of it. At the beach I curled my toes under the sand to hide it. In gym class, at the pool, sitting on the bleachers, I curled my toes inward on top of the floor just to hide it. I did this little curling action everywhere else I went barefoot, just to hide the yellow toenail, and the insecurity. With others, for example, if I was in a hot tub and a bunch of us were sitting in our own corner, jets on or off, they would say, "Get that thing out of the water!"

I asked my father, "Why is my toenail yellow?"

He said, "It's toenail fungus."

That was all that I learned about it, all that I knew, for a long time...

Chapter 16

One day I went to the doctor's office. The appointment was for an annual physical, to document some statistics in a booklet. My eyesight was tested, using a wooden spoon to cover one eye, then reading the letters on a poster with the other. I had very good vision, luckily, and knowing that made me happy.

"20/15," the doctor said. "Good job."

In the room he pressed a cold metal object, as I inhaled and exhaled, all over my back. Then, after examining other parts of my body, and even feeling a bit anxious, I was asked if I had any concerns or questions, or if anything was bothering me.

"My toenail has fungus," I said. "Why?"

At this point my little shoes and socks were off and the doctor was examining the middle toe on my left foot. "Well," he said. "We can make it better."

"Thank you," I said.

That day I was prescribed an antifungal medication. It was a pill and I was instructed to take it once a day, I believe, for three months. Then three months later the yellow toenail was gone. It had grown out from the roots normally. Every couple of weeks when I or even one of my parents cut my toenails, little by little, it cleared up. Eventually, all of my toenails were normal, somewhat translucent, opaque, no longer yellowish. The feeling was, liberating. I went around barefoot just because it felt, very good, being free of insecurities. Gym class was all right; I walked around the pool area a bit more freely. One evening, my friend's mother said at the dinner table, "Andy's built like a wrestler." So, I thought of that from time to time, instead of worrying about the yellow toenail.

A couple of months went by. On Halloween, I went trick-or-treating and ate some candy. On Thanksgiving, I said thanks and had some stuffing. Then, before all the holiday decorations went up, I came down with strep throat.

It happened overnight. I went to bed and felt normal. Maybe I had a slight tickle on the back of my throat. It was light though, untroubling. But then in the morning, it felt rough. Just swallowing, that basic reflex, was painful. Eating and drinking at that moment was a problem. I tried chicken noodle soup, it hurt; warm milk, same thing. So, I went to the doctor's office.

There I was swabbed, right on the back of the throat, which was worse than any reflex, eating, or drinking. The doctor said that it was indeed strep throat but still took the swab to the lab. I hardly had to wait. It was a different doctor than the last time, but I knew her, and she came back right away with the results.

"That was the quick," she said. "That means it's a bad case of strep throat."

Back then I said, "Okay." But now, I'm thinking, it's kind of interesting, she had been my neighbor by chance. And she was the first person to say, during that visit, "You have a high pain tolerance."

And then she wrote out a prescription: antibiotics.

I took this medication very briefly. Either the infection cleared or I just felt better after a day or two. But I followed the instructions and took the antibiotics for about a week. I stayed at the house for a couple of days. I always liked staying inside at that time of year, before other insecurities or familial issues arose. I maybe even started taking notes then, just in my mind, little notes, little thoughts and ideas, figuring out the world and what it is.

Then, the yellow toenail came back, same foot, same toe. I went back to the doctor's office, and I tried the same antifungal medication, but it did not work. It appeared the infection, or really the fungi, had developed a resistance to the medication. So, I went with the yellow toenail for a while.

Everything was still the same, I just curled my toes under my foot, I wore socks, rarely went barefoot, just as before. It was not bad... It was actually a decent time of year, wonderful even, nearing spring. There was snow on the ground, and there were frequent snow squalls, a few storms. The neighborhood kids invited me over and at least at one neighbor's house we went into his hot tub almost daily. It was usually at night, especially while snowing.

The hot tub was on the back porch. We went outside through the sunroom, which was full of exotic plants that I enjoyed touching and just being around, like ficus trees and peace lilies and perhaps even orchids, so inside that room it had to be warm, and then outside we walked lightly clothed across the frozen boards, fast. All around was snow, and that might seem restrictive, it almost always was, but in the hot tub it was not. We sometimes got out of the hot tub and then ran out and dove into the snow. And then we ran back through the snow and climbed into the hot tub, and what a tingling, sensational shock. The water was set at around 104°F. Getting back into the hot tub, coming straight from the snow, the water felt much warmer than that. Then it was pleasant. If it was nighttime and the lights were on, and if it was snowing and the flakes were illuminated in the light, floating so freely near the bulbs, it was very pleasant. But still, referring to the yellow toenail, I heard, "Get that thing out of the water!"

So I ran out into the snow, then went back and sat in the hot tub, but positioned my leg out of the water and somewhat uncomfortably hanging over the edge of the tub. I had to. I was that vulnerable—like a cell phone being tapped. And things went on that way, not all the time, but only when I was barefoot. It was not a bad thing, but only one little thing, actually. It was just a yellow toenail, for now.

Chapter 17

I went to a friend's lake house in the summer. I stayed there for many days, and we were always active, swimming, hiking, kayaking, playing badminton. For some reason I didn't take a shower. I thought that swimming in the water was enough. I was getting washed, even with very pure water, but not cleaned. Then, after a few days, my friend noticed the first flake in my hair. It might have been a bit startling, maybe, "What is that?"

He picked it out and we examined it, a small flake, almost like skin that peels after a sun burn or a scab, but different. He looked again, but this time more thoroughly by parting my hair, and he found a few more. They were small flakes, but great, golden flakes. I thought, first it's the yellow toenail, then my throat, now these kind of flakes, are they connected; or, what's next?

"I don't know," I said. And even wearing shoes, I still curled my toes in.

That was under the sun, with warm, even moist conditions. Come fall the flakes were finer, not as sparse, and paler. But, after getting the right shampoo, they cleared up right away.

Then toward early winter I came down with strep throat again, and for a few consecutive winters, it was the same thing. I remembered during previous winters getting the whooping cough, and also the croup cough, several times. It was bad. My immune system was busy, but not as strong as the body and mind. I heard it in the cough—it sounded harsh, almost like a bark. It was a strong force from within, and I was sick as a dog, until it cleared up. After experiencing both coughs multiple times, my immune system probably got used to the infections. Or maybe it learned to endure them, then fight them off. I sometimes sat thinking, why me?

For a while there was a cycle to these problems. Summer it was one infection, fall was another, same with winter, and so was spring. All year round it was the yellow toenail. And I was still eager, enthusiastic, a good boy, externally. But internally I always seemed to be fighting off or enduring something. It was an ongoing process of taking antibiotics or some other medication, then feeling better, and sometime later, feeling worse, then fighting off or enduring something else. What I did not know was that these antibiotics and medications can disrupt internal homeostasis. They might provide temporary relief, but over time they can produce some adverse effects. It is possible that they can affect the balance of organisms living in your body. During homeostasis, when there is a balance of internal organisms, everything is good. But I already had an imbalance of microbiota. And medications like antibiotics not only kill the bad bacteria, causing the infection, but also the good bacteria. So, from a young age I was more prone to infection, and I had a higher risk of developing more serious or painful conditions.

The cycle continued, between strep throat and both coughs and the yellow toenail and the flakes. At some point as a kid, the infections causing some of these ailments stopped. I no longer came down with strep throat, the croup cough, or the whooping cough, but the fungal infection persisted. I still had the yellow toenail, and the flakes occasionally came back late fall and early winter. Then sometime before turning ten years old, I must have outgrown the other infections of the respiratory tract. My body possibly learned how to fight them off, maybe by growing resistant to them, solving problems and outgrowing one phase or another.

Chapter 18

My visits to the doctor's office decreased, but I still went for the annual checkup.

I had noticed that while wearing pants, particularly pants that were tight around the waist, there was some stomach pain. It varied in intensity depending on how tight the pants were and what food I had recently consumed, if any. Things usually felt best between meals at the house, and worst after meals at school, especially in the winter. That time of year I wore pants, and they were usually jeans that felt too small, though they were the right size. After lunch, the pain, an internal, abdominal pain that is hard to describe, was most noticeable. I figured that it was something I ate, and it happened after almost every meal that I ate. Part of this pain or discomfort seemed to be my gut trying to expand as though it were inflamed, and in fact it was inflamed, but it was unable to expand because of the tight pants. The pants were not normally tight, but after eating, the inflammation added some, additional, girth, making them feel tight.

Then there were the after-school sports, practices, games, having to wear uniform pants that were of course normally tight. I remember running up and down the field, or standing in the field, or even just sitting on the bench; there was always at least a slight degree of abdominal discomfort. It varied, and so did I, each day. I was pretty good at most sports even with the pain. But it affected my performance, or rather my feeling, my competitive spirit, or lack thereof. This pain, the discomfort, was the competition, that was the battle. I was just battling myself, not the other team, or even the textbooks in school. But had I felt all right in those uniform pants, and also in those distinctly tight jeans, I would have been a much better athlete and student, a happier person, or at least more so on the inside, all day. However, the moment that I went back to that house and changed into something more comfortable, or nothing at all, I felt great. Otherwise, I felt slightly pained, some discomfort, and I thought that that was normal.

After school one day I went to the doctor's office for an annual checkup. It was my last appointment with a pediatrician, sometime in the winter between sports, and I just happened to be wearing a pair of those tight pants. I had been wearing them all day, and for lunch I'd had some food that was high in sugar, as usual. So, at the doctor's office there was definitely some discomfort. This time there was a new doctor. Over the course of ten years there had been three or four doctors, and one was my neighbor, but she had retired early, I believe, and then moved to another house. The new doctor was kind, seemed caring, had great attention for anything that might be wrong, any possible discomfort, or condition. We went through the normal procedures, except for a few. I had to ask to get my eyesight tested, and my vision was still good. Then I lay on the exam table, socks off, and I could see the yellow toenail. Even then I curled my toes in. The doctor pressed down on my upper abdomen, close to my chest, and said nothing. It felt normal to me, and probably to him as well. He moved around my abdomen, applying pressure quietly, and then closer to my waist, he must have found a potential problem. He pressed down, and he kept pressing down, but lightly.

"Does that feel tender or uncomfortable?"

Then, "Does it hurt?"

"No," I said. But it did.

It felt tender, or else like a knot, but so uniquely, I do not know how to compare the feeling to something else. Pressing down, lightly as it was, could have felt like getting punched in the stomach, but I don't know how it feels to get punched in the stomach with a normal stomach. Only getting hit in the stomach while playing football might compare. But those pants! I knew that there was a problem, that likely something was wrong, but I couldn't do much out of anxiousness, and the abdominal discomfort caused anxiousness. This cycle had a fairly negative effect, I figured out, at least on perception. Vision was good, but emotions could have had a different meaning. What excitement felt like for one person could have been much different than the excitement that I felt—or any other feeling, because of the discomfort.

I kept the same habits, eating and drinking poorly, probably a lot of sugar, and much more of it than I was aware of. Sweet foods taste good, and I feel good, in the moment. But also, unbeknownst to me, these sugars were feeding the infection inside me, just enough to keep the fungi and bad bacteria, which everyone has, overgrown and active. These organisms had already experienced an overgrowth, but without the right conditions, enough stress, stronger medications, it was not quite an extreme overgrowth, yet. So the cycle continued. I just managed it well.

The doctor stood back. I sat up on the edge of the table.

"Is there anything else that you would like me to look at?"

I thought about the yellow toenail. Curling my toes in, my legs dangled so freely.

I cannot remember what happened after that, but later in the day I wore some loose-fitting clothes and felt better. I slept soundly, then got up early, ready for the day.

Chapter 19

During middle school there were more problems. I have already written about them in a book, *Any Moment*. So right now, it might be more like an overview. But these problems caused some insecurities, and they certainly affected my own problems.

My brother began experiencing a side effect that is totally uncommon, if it is even known, of a medication used to treat many diseases and conditions associated with inflammation. For him, it was a serious skin rash, and he experienced an adverse reaction not to the skin but to the mind. It was so serious that he took other medications, like anti-depressants, to try and help. But it was not depression that caused him to suddenly change. It's unknow what the reaction caused. Whatever it was, it might not have fallen under the umbrella of symptoms for that disorder, and the other medications used to treat this disorder only made the whole problem worse for him. It was very stressful, especially at that house, but stressful does not do that setting justice. Seeing a family member hurt, or anyone else for that matter, also hurt me. I withdrew to avoid all the problems, and by doing so it made mine noticeably worse. His stress made my parents stressed which made me stressed. And again, stress. I don't know if that's just for the situation and setting. But sticking with just stress, this was when I first realized that stress exacerbates the problem, and that my stomach felt worse, there was more pain, and combined with all the problems, the effect on emotions, like happiness, or excitement, was even more noticeable, harder to properly feel. So, to feel better, I continued eating poorly. I fed the cycle, and though a year or two later I improved my diet and in fact felt better, I still noticed some unpleasant reactions to the food that I ate. For now, and for a little while longer, I ate anything that tasted good. It was mostly food that was high in sugar, and much of the time my lower abdomen felt inflamed. However, I did not take a medication for the inflammation. It hurt, but only on the inside.

The insecurities were different. I was unaccustomed to them. I still had the yellow toenail, and toward the end of fall or early winter, occasionally some flakes. But they all evolved around the same feeling, not really knowing what it might be, then knowing what it was. So I seldom had people over to that house, and when I did, there were only a few, but even then I almost felt embarrassed, because of that house. It was different than the other insecurities. Maybe I was not used to it. It was unlike the yellow toenail and the flakes, where I just showered and put on socks afterward.

Everything might have seemed abnormal from an early point. It was, especially this part of it, at least. But other things were for the most part normal, at that age and in that grade. I went over to other people's houses, we explored the land, competed in sports, and also in school, sat around tables at lunch, then went to those dances.

Once, when I went over to someone's house after a dance, we watched a movie starring one of the great American actors. He said, "Get off my lawn." Then realized, like my cell phone, *but it's unlocked...* Making a movie with him was just a dream. And *my thought.*

The three of us went down into my friend's basement after the movie. I finally changed into something comfortable. At the dance, I wore a pair of elegant pants and they felt normal there, or at least my stomach did, and I even felt great. I believe that I did not eat before the dance. Yet I had plenty of energy. Most people stood around in small circles. I ran on the wall, literally. I got almost the opposite of a head start. The wall had padding and I took several strides horizontally along the pads and then arched down and joined another circle. Chaperones watched this boho doing—something. They had never seen it before, but it was surprising to see, even wonderful. I felt better than usual, that was all, and I thought that I looked dapper in those pants. Then later I had something to eat, and whatever it was, I immediately felt different. It was not an unusual feeling, but it was heavier than normal. The pants seemed one or two sizes too small. I no longer felt as light as I had, at the dance, but a little heavy. I sat on the couch, relaxed. The movie helped tremendously.

In the basement, wearing something more comfortable, the heaviness then released. Inside it had been only hot air, in the bowels, then the passage of all this air went off at once. It was marvelous, and once was not enough. It was actually one after the other, because inside, a lot had built up. Afterward, I felt much better, and the night went on, normally.

Chapter 20

How soon the situation became heavier. Problems at that house were much more serious. There were hospitalizations and my brother was the patient. My parents went and I stayed at the house. I won't go into detail; all that happened or how. I don't really like talking about it when the issues were not mine, they were my brother's, and like I said, I have already written about them in *Any Moment,* but nothing could capture or recreate all those moments. The medications that he took, which were for a disorder that he probably did not have, affected his mood, emotions, and really, everything.

There was more stress at that house, and when I was there, I typically went down in the basement and kept to myself. More often I went out with other kids, usually because we had nothing else to do, and I had a good reason to get out of the house. But they were probably antsy too. It was a good thing to do, maybe even important. It is part of going through changes, and this one was without stress and suffering, which can alter beings. Then I began to notice that more and more foods upset and caused stress to my stomach. I thought that it was just because the foods were unhealthy, not that the problem might be caused by certain ingredients in the foods. These are separate problems. But, maybe, the problem was a little of both.

One thing I found that helped was running. It might have been why I felt great at that dance. There I was running on the walls, and all of that activity got things moving on the inside. Once I stopped and ate, the heavy feeling came back. It was almost the same on the sports field. I got into those pants and felt distended, but running around I felt, maybe, normal. Then during rests, and sometimes after eating a snack, that heavy feeling came back. I wondered, if only I felt normal all the time, how would it then feel to, run around?

I went with Ricky and some others to an outdoor shopping center. It was nighttime, between seasons. There were leaves on the ground and a few blowing in the wind: a clear night, the moon glowed fully.

"What do you guys want to do?"

"Get a good steak?"

"Go on a trip…"

We went inside an old chain restaurant and were seated at a table. It had cloth that draped squarely over the sides, reaching nearly to the floor, and soon on top stood several glasses of water. The menu was well-illustrated. Most dishes were fairly inexpensive. We ordered many different appetizers, waited, table set. Then there was food, and next we feasted…

It seemed like after the meal, under the moon and the starry night, the feeling of heaviness inside could only be compared to the strange feeling after putting a shirt on backwards. That was how I thought of it then, and it was perceived right away, like, what's going on? Would I enjoy walking around all day with a shirt on backwards? That was before it became painful. That problem has a simple solution, taking my shirt off, but this problem was touchy, deep, and not so simple. It was not only unusual, abnormal, but also complex.

I thought of only one thing to do, and that was to physically run. Ricky commented maybe on the quickness, or that it might have been random, but it was not. There was good reason to running down main street as I was; running not toward the moon, but under the moon and the stars toward the night; running because it was a rush, I felt great, and great was normal, but normal was not great.

And then, the night ended. I went down in the basement. The problems were there, familial problems, upstairs. But my socks were on, shirt was forwards, I think. I had showered and still felt all right, another day, another night.

Chapter 21

The struggle inside remained ongoing. My brother had his issues. And I kept mine to myself. Staying active of course helped. Moving around, just being in motion, alleviated the problem.

Luckily some friends invited me to go skiing often. I went with them to their condos, at least for a weekend, and sometimes for a whole week or longer. I got to escape the problems at that house, and in turn, my problems felt better. Away from the familial problems, I experienced less stress internally. My stomach and that whole surrounding area felt relaxed, and so did my mind and spirit. That was experienced even just driving to the mountain, being away from the problems and knowing that I will be away from them for at least a little while—and then actually moving around on the mountain!

In the summer, a group of us went on a trip there, and one day we went on a hike. I am getting ahead of myself in chronology. When we were first introduced to cannabis, which I found had a helpful effect, that happened before this trip. But on the trip, without it, hiking the mountain was especially soothing. Then afterward, we went to a river and I went for a swim. I dove off a rock into a deep pool of water, and it felt refreshing, then moving around freely was even more invigorating.

Skiing, we always worked up a great appetite. When I started going to the mountain regularly, that was when substances first occasionally entered the picture. It is important to mention them, cannabis and alcohol, because both alleviated the abdominal discomfort, and we only occasionally had one or the other at night. It is important to note this. We did not consume them often; how they alleviated the discomfort was just an observation, and a good reason to look forward to the occasion.

One of those nights we went out to dinner. After skiing all day and going through the woods and off jumps and over moguls I felt great, or in other words, normal. Knowing that this was one of those occasions, I ordered a, specialty, hamburger. It had this savory sauce that was delicious. It was not the first time that I had ordered it. My friend knew about the troubles that it caused.

"Oh," he said. "The scusi sauce?"

Just after one bite; but it was so good.

Then after one sip; it tasted even better.

And soon… I felt better, much better.

Chapter 22

That year playing baseball there was another semi disturbance. It lasted only while wearing the uniform, and only after chewing gum, until I took off the uniform. The bus rides home after games are almost as memorable as playing the sport itself for this reason, the heaviness, that backwards feeling.

My team was good. We were solid ball players. I put some baseball moments in *Any Moment*, because I liked just playing the sport, but I never described much of the discomfort that I played through, if at all.

A lot of teammates chewed sunflower seeds. I did as well, though really preferred gum. It was the sugar in the gum that I liked, the sweetness of that substance. Chewing on something was something to do between pitches. But something else built up inside, causing abdominal distension, and much more than any other meal or food had. I ran around the diamond, chased fly balls, warmed up, pitched, and outwardly, hardly noticed the distension. My performance, as far as I knew, was unaffected and better than most; thinking that the discomfort was normal. Then, after stopping this activity and sitting down, I saw how the process developed and continued. Chewing on the gum produced a lot of saliva, a lot of small air bubbles, and I swallowed the saliva and all of that air, and then it built up inside, but none of it passed because of the pants!

I remember riding on the busses after games, even after a win, feeling discontented. I had to loosen my belt and pants to experience any relief, and it was incredible. But the internal problems seemed to be growing, getting worse.

It was during the football season of my second year in high school when I experienced my first serious illness since the days of getting strep throat and the croup and whooping coughs. It developed almost overnight. At the end of practice, I felt slightly more fatigued than normal, but after showering at the house, I put on some comfortable clothing and felt, better. I thought that it was probably just a cold, and that it might pass on its own quickly, or at least I hoped that it would.

I went to bed and in the morning woke up with small red spots on both of my hands. I felt drained. Any other time of year I would have stayed home sick. But it was football season, I never missed a practice or a game. I felt drained, but normally the abdominal discomfort had a similar effect. Together it was very ailing.

Plus, I had those red spots on my hands. Throughout the day I put them in my pockets. And then the headache!

I was more quiet than usual all day. Practice that afternoon focused on defense. There were a lot of drills and we ran a lot. I often nearly collapsed, just because of this illness, its effect was so strong. I thought that my immune system had finally improved, but it had not...

The next day, it was even worse, debilitating. The red spots had formed into these small callus-like blisters on my hands. I had gone to bed early, could hardly stay awake. In health class I just happened to come across the exact infection in the textbook. It had the name of the infection, its symptoms, a picture of a hand with those small red spots, then another with the callus-like blisters. I learned a little from reading about it in that textbook, though much more from experiencing it. But, right after class I forgot what it was called.

My mind was very slow that day. I could not focus on the lecture, which was why I browsed through the textbook for the answer.

Another problem, of course, had to do with the stomach. There was discomfort, but with this infection it hurt. Before practice I went to the bathroom and heaved. It was a cold rainy day on the field. I had never experienced such awful chills or fatigue.

I told no one about it. In fact, it did not even affect me on the field, seemingly. I might have even been better, and that could have had something to do with, another trait passed down from our ancestors. What, "fight-or-flight."

And the whistle blew. We ran, ran, then stopped.

Over the weekend it cleared up. Everything went back to, normal.

Chapter 23

The yellow toenail issue continued. It might have even altered the present moment; the way things stand right now.

Without the yellow toenail, and the other issues, I would have been happier, more confident. I went to the mountain with George many times that winter. We skied, played basketball, practiced football, talked big, and loafed around with other people. The word loaf is, in part, the name of the mountain, and there were a few inground hot tubs around the base of it that we soaked in occasionally. The warm water had a very relaxing effect on my being, as well as just talking, even between minds. The girls were there, and instead of thinking dreamily, but presently, I was probably thinking of something else. It might have been about the yellow toenail, the scusi sauce, my stomach, and the other issues, somewhat described in other books, at that house. That's why I was so self-contained.

What could have been would have changed everything.

A few months later, after a dentist appointment, my wisdom teeth were pulled out. I wondered beforehand about the name of those teeth. I'd been wise for a while, at this point, from knowledge, innatism, and these teeth were just coming in then? It was likely because of the problem.

Pulling them out caused some soreness. I took the prescribed pain medications and things felt better. There was still half of the bottle left after things had healed, and it might still be in that medicine cabinet now, right next to that sink, and behind that was the fridge, to the side was the oven, it was that kitchen.

My gums felt better before the weekend. I went to a restaurant and ate some chicken wings. Before that weekend, I had been able to tolerate this kind of food, pretty well, considering the reactions that I had to some other foods. In fact, I enjoyed spicy food. It had no more of an internal effect than almost anything else that I ate, and in a way, because of the burn, spicy foods were better. Everyone else avoided these foods because they do trigger pain, but combined with the discomfort that I was already experiencing, this added sensation almost complimented it, or better yet, masked it. This is not random; it could have been like squeezing a loved one's hand while experiencing pain; only my condition somehow masked the emotion, and being hard to perceive, that coincidentally made it much more desirable, but so out of reach, I had only my other hand to grab.

In any case, after getting my wisdom teeth pulled out and then recovering from that procedure, some foods that had normally been tolerable then became troublesome. Eating it was the same as before, but digesting it caused some problems. I hiccupped and some of this spicy matter went up the wrong pipe, but only to my chest. It had a sour burning sensation and stayed there for a while. Even when this reflex went away, the sensation continued, and the longer it did, the worse it got. It was tolerable, but unpleasant. Not the reflex, but acid reflux.

I wondered if it was the stress, operation, medication, my immune system, that condition… probably a combination. It was a strange hill to climb.

Football was another. But for conditioning, we actually ran up hills. We practiced throughout the summer, and during that time, we did not usually play through the rain but almost always everything else, and sometimes the grass was wet. I sweat a lot, and so did my feet, inside my cleats. They usually felt damp, and I always left them outside to dry after practice, and then I showered. But, unfortunately, one time after practice I noticed that the toenail on my big toe appeared slightly yellow. Fungi thrive in damp environments. I figured

77

that out, but the wondering continued. Was it just the cleats; or, by chance, did it start happening after the operation, then the reflux?

My mind was preoccupied with this, these problems, while those around me preoccupied themselves with, maybe the whole machine. So it seemed natural to think about other, even worldly problems; but experiencing my own made it hard to understand those or these.

Then, one weekend my best friend had an open house, and a few people over. I was wearing sandals, which was unusual for me. My shoes as well as my cleats must have both been damp, drying out. I never went around barefoot, flashing my toe, as it were. I studied it as the others focused on the TV. The big toenail was just beginning to yellow, and the middle toenail was not only yellow, but then, also thick.

I thought that there had to be an explanation. It was not just an anomaly.

There was talking, and there was also commentary on the TV. Then the door opened and my scientific bubble popped. She came into the room, and then I curled my toes in, was quiet.

Like, "Hey, I'd like to be myself around you."

But, "I feel silly and diffident and eager, combined."

Yes, "Together."

Oh, much better. Even the problems, or really having the problems, in a way seemed wonted.

Chapter 24

A couple of months later I injured my knee. It happened on the football field during a scrimmage, and it was almost expected, just a matter of when and how. I made a regular play on defense and going down to the ground my ACL and meniscus tore. This of course is better described in *Any Moment*. There was some pain at first, so I limped off the field and iced my knee, then watched the rest of the scrimmage from a good spot on the sideline. Not long after that I got an MRI, which was really when I learned about the injuries, what they were, and that I had to get surgery. About a week later I did.

Recovering from the surgery itself was obviously much more prolonged and stressful than recovering from the dental operation. The whole area around my knee felt very, very sore. I certainly needed the pain medication, and aside from some of the noticeable side effects, they alleviated the soreness. I did not feel very smart, but I did not feel much pain or stress either, and they also had a positive effect on the abdominal discomfort.

But, as soon as I stopped taking the medication, even though my knee felt better, the discomfort seemed worse. Acid reflux occurred more often, but cannabis helped with this condition, the discomfort, and with the recovery. The whole injury and recovery was, in a way, a special occasion with medicine. It was an unfortunate incident no doubt, not a big event or injury, but a somewhat common injury, and this kind of help was appropriate.

Things were fairly good for a while. I only had some help while recovering, in terms of cannabis, but not much, and my knee fully healed—quite fast. In four months, after getting the surgery, I was skiing and playing sports again. Things were almost back to normal, only there was more abdominal discomfort than there had been before. There was still a problem consuming some foods, and though consuming cannabis had been beneficial and helpful just a few months earlier, medicinally, for a while, on those special occasions, it seemed to make the problem inside worse, even though it was not the problem. The root of the problem was internal.

I began to notice that it had a similar effect to chewing gum while playing baseball. In the process of consumption, air sort of leaked down into my stomach and caused distension. At that point, the feeling was familiar but just as hard to tolerate as before, if not harder. The inner distension that it caused was worse. It was because instead of relieving stress, which normally it had, and which made it special on those occasions, it caused stress, and stress made the inflammation inside worse, then all the air caused pressure and pain.

So, there was another cycle, another problem, another hill to climb. This one had an easy answer, just stop consumption. That kind of special occasion had to, momentarily, stop. But it would only be temporary, I thought. I bounced back easily from injuries then, and I hoped that in this instance, it would be just as easy.

Chapter 25

But there were more stressful events. Being 17 with a lot to carry under the surface is the simple, even logical explanation for their happening, though a closer look would show that all the other problems at that time were also responsible; I had to grow up fast. And I think that is the simple explanation of the closer look.

These events or some of them that happened when I was 17 are somewhat explained and better described in *Any Moment*. The descriptions of them are not too in depth, and unlike this book, the internal problems are not at all explained. Literarily, it might be known as the iceberg theory, writing about an event, what happened, as it was seen and experienced, and as though it were happening again in that moment. But because it had already happened, and associations had already been made, there is much more under the surface, under the iceberg that cannot be seen, that describes how the event came to be, how it happened, and possibly why.

So, the iceberg theory. There is much more under the surface than what can be seen. Like memory. And it was like my stomach, but on the inside, what could only be felt.

In *Any Moment*, I used this technique to write the majority of the book. I described those events as they appeared in memory, not only because I enjoy the technique, in writing, and applying it myself, but also for a reason... Think about all the different subjects that great American writers have written about. Questioning one's suffering and pain, happiness, brain, that could be taken personally. And many events that have happened too just feel personal.

At least a few stressful experiences happened at 17, not including the situation at that house. It was not a good year, and for maybe half of it, aside from academics and extracurriculars, I was often in the basement at that house.

Toward the end of the winter and through the summer I was very busy. There was school, then work after school, and then practice after work, and work on the weekends. It was at work when I noticed that the problem inside felt the worst, the most painful, feeling so afflicted, almost being unable to work. We were very active there, always moving around, and movement had helped the problem in the past, which was hard to understand at first. Would external factors affect internal problems, or was it just the work, working through pain to support the pain?

I rarely complained or at least voiced the discomfort. If I did, whatever it was about had to be quite bad, and when I did, it was usually about the same thing I said, "Aw, my stomach…"

I thought of the times when doing recreational activities was just to have fun, and though they were still the same and that was still the case at that time, there was more of an urge because doing these things masked or even stopped the pain.

Playing basketball, for example, the ball nearly grew wings. All the discomfort went away. I ran around the court, shot, scored, and scoring felt good. I played tennis sometimes and occasionally golfed on a day off. Being active helped a lot, though at work the discomfort always came back. It got pretty intense, and when it did, I tended to say that my stomach felt "contorted." By this I meant that it felt so distended the correct medical term might be "volvulus." Otherwise, I thought that there was inner distension and inflammation and perhaps some kind of imbalance. I took some supplements but I didn't notice much of a difference. Yet I could still see the beauty of the world around, however dimmed, and was living, and really thriving, off the hope that things would get better, better, not worse…

Chapter 26

I went to college almost insecure because the yellow toenail seemed thicker and the infection had spread fully to the big toenail and the smallest toenail on my left foot, though somewhat minimally. I first noticed that the infection was spreading after getting my wisdom teeth pulled out, and at that time I also frequently wore damp cleats, the kind of environment that fungi thrive in, but that was when it first started. After getting knee surgery, the infection continued to spread, and there were many more instances of wearing wet, damp shoes, and cleats. In two years, the infection had spread to two additional toenails. It was frustrating.

Then, there were the dormitory showers. They were cleaned regularly, but I thought that they were likely, rather, unclean. There were probably around 50 or 100 males living on the floor that I lived on, and on any given day that number could have easily been doubled or tripled, because people from other floors or other dorm halls or even other schools were frequently there, somewhere on the floor. The ones who did not live on the floor were almost always the ones who made a mess in the bathroom, and it was easy to tell because they never flushed or cleaned up afterward, which I could never understand. There was one bathroom shared between fifty to over a hundred college freshman. It had several toilets and in most of them, especially on weekends, there were many different kinds of matter, at least in the bowl, and sometimes around the seat and the floor. It was gross. Some people complained. We had floor-wide meetings. But the inconsiderate conduct continued. So, I wore sandals even in the shower. All other times I wore shoes, and sometimes, just socks.

The bathroom might have been the worst during the first week there. It was on a weeknight when I sort of witnessed one of these incidents. A few years later I heard a similar story, and I thought that it was amusing then, but that night it was much more frustrating. I went into the bathroom to take a shower at around 9:00pm, opened the door, and there was someone standing in front of the mirror, sleeping. He woke up, and as I went into a shower, he went into one of the bathroom stalls. I could hear the unpleasant sounds through the white noise of running water, and then in the morning there was a bit of a mess in multiple stalls. It became something that everyone got used to, in my case, like most insecurities, except for issues at that house.

Three weeks into the semester there was another stressful experience, and this one is better detailed in my first or third book, *The One*. In short, it was one of those special occasions, having some cannabis one night, and I do not believe that it should have been an arrestable offense. That's probably in that first book, and there are probably more explanations why it was underneath the surface, reasons for reform that are part of the iceberg, even though I know that the ocean goes much deeper. Since that experience, I believe that laws were changed; it would not happen again, being arrested from being around cannabis. But it did happen then, and all throughout the experience, from that night until the case was resolved, I noticed much more abdominal discomfort than what had been, normal.

There might have been another factor that contributed to this as well. The university food, which was pretty good and had been voted as some of the best around, was hard to digest. And, by the way the bathroom looked, it might have even been troublesome. I had heard, whether it's true or not, that the food contained added laxatives; possibly, if that was the case, to prevent foodborne illnesses. I don't know if the food actually had any added substances to stimulate the bowels or not, but I did notice more discomfort after eating it. If laxatives were in fact present, it would have had a similar internal effect to the medications that were taken after surgery. Both might be harmful internally, which is a reason why they should not be consumed long-term. Yet every meal I ate the food, and if that myth was the case, it was long-term.

Throughout the stressful experience, I often felt abdominal pain, especially after eating. I had the usual foods, not knowing that some of the foods were possibly causing irritation, or that maybe these foods were being improperly digested, and I did not realize that it was probably a combination of that, the food, and the stress, the pain.

However, academically, I did quite well that semester. I made the dean's list and into the papers, for that.

It might have been that under stress I worked the best. Maybe not *the* best, but better without pain. That was always the case. Whether or not what I did was the best that I could do, it was always a trying effort, because suffering, I had to give extra effort to do anything, and get anything done. In that regard, though stress was detrimental, it might have also been helpful in a way. This could have been because of that ancestral trait, the fight-or-flight instinct, a natural response to stressful situations.

There are plenty of those out there in the world, and they're all different. Those that I experienced, altogether, were definitely different. But, the insecurities!

Chapter 27

Did I do anything to combat the stress or discomfort, that abdominal pain? I believe I did, but there was only so much that I could do, yet it turned out to be a lot. I still had to eat, so I still experienced discomfort. The food was pleasurable, but once it reached the stomach there was often pain. However, I stayed inside most nights, and most days I felt at least a little better. I have written some fairly good passages late at night. Plus, what might be considered late at night in one part of the world, in another part of the world it could be daytime, and for all I know, that day, a peace treaty was signed. So, at any time of day or night, good things can happen, and there can always be some discomfort.

Focusing on work, one project, assignment, or another, also helped. Many people actually asked for help, and by staying in at night, though not always, I was readily available.

Although I went to school for business and even took a liking to art at an early age, I saw all kinds of problems relating to many different subjects. And even through the haze, caused by the discomfort, each one and its respective solution or configuration clearly stood out. Then, they went back to work more understanding, and so did I. While dealing with the discomfort, it was, in a sense, a good deal. It was like working with one accord, someone else and I, toward an accord.

Luckily, far fewer stressful events occurred during that time, the end of winter through spring. Early winter was a sad time that year, and later, at work, there was indeed some summertime stress. Yet it was summertime, and I was 19 years old. My body had only been slightly scathed and restored at that point—knee surgery. And even my knee felt mostly normal, besides some scar tissue around the joint, it functioned the same as it always had—satisfactorily. But my stomach, not so much, that had a mind of its own. Every day that I went into work I knew that there would be some pain. It affected my mind, of course, maybe even tastebuds, or sugar cravings. It caused stress, and that caused pain.

Well, I was only 19. I was grounded, but sometimes I got swept off my feet, and other times the distension dimmed my mind, though that was a reason why it worked so sharply; it took extra power to brighten the picture.

Chapter 28

Not long after returning to campus in the fall, and after being enrolled in several foundational business courses, I thought more and more abstractly, and more and more I desired to write a book. The idea of being a writer was appealing, in part because I watched a show based on a writer and I thought that it was interesting. He was good, and he certainly had his share of difficult times. An idea came to his mind and then he wrote it down, and best of all, he had a team. That must make things easy, but I figured it must only be in Hollywood.

The idea came to my mind while standing out on a balcony, talking to someone about economics. It was their generalized area of study, and I thought, that must good, feel good too.

I knew that I had a story to write, ideas to get down, a lot to let out, and in a way that is different. But every time that an idea popped up, and it could have been an abstract idea just as well as a simple idea—while I was getting ahead of myself, feeling almost unsure about a book's inception from one idea—the abdominal discomfort sort of obscured the idea. Then, for a while, the notion of writing a book was only just an idea. It seemed like all that I could do mentally at that time was remember terms never before seen, connect dots, and understand concepts, but making my own seemed like too much, effort.

Things being what they were, being on the cusp of a great task; in hindsight, some big event had to occur to onset the transitional phase.

Sometime later that fall, things in memory now start to seem fuzzy, and these memories get even fuzzier as the weather began to change. I had been eating that food for a while, and the gut sensations increased. Overtime, though the visual memories have become fuzzier, my gut feeling has remained clear in memory; at that time, my gut felt bad.

Then, one night, I made a blunder. Not only does my memory of that night seem fuzzy now, and fuzzier as time goes on, I believe that that night my mind was fuzzy too. I know that my abdomen hurt, it was carrying a lot of pain, and my hypothesis of why this is important is included just a little later in part 2 of this book. It was formed by a different self, examining the actions of a past self; two separate beings, I believe.

Anyway, that blunder; I was inside a department store after it had closed, and then I was arrested, seriously charged, and booked.

The whole event is described in depth in my book, *The One*. I was arrested that night, and afterward, although I was upset, the feeling in my gut was no different than it had been for the past, decade, maybe. But my stomach, my gut, said something or almost sensed something completely different. It was kind of like clairvoyance. Like, *Any Moment*…

About a week later I suffered nearly fatal injuries at college, one being a severe traumatic brain injury, which caused amnesia and is why my memory, leading up to these events, has always seemed fuzzy. Then a week later, unaware that the events had even occurred, I woke up from a coma in the intensive care unit at a hospital. I was in Boston, but if I had not been told where I was almost immediately, it could have been anywhere, waking up somewhere, coming back to life. My mind was especially fuzzy, and my body hurt, but my stomach felt all right.

Chapter 29

For the next two weeks in the hospital I experienced very little distension. I took many pain medications for the injuries—fractures mostly, to the spine, skull, ribs, pelvis, and some had to be surgically repaired. All of this was because I fell 50 feet onto ice, and even though I have no memory of what happened and the investigation was insufficient, I believe that something very bad happened that night, of course. It is described more in *The One*, but that was what I remembered then, when I wrote it, but now after more time has passed and other serious events and ordeals have occurred, I remember less.

During those two weeks, in the intensive care unit, I seldom felt abdominal discomfort because of the pain medications. Then I stopped taking them and it returned, along with intense back pain. The latter went away completely about a few months after the ordeal took place, but the gut discomfort worsened.

I kept most of this out of the first book, *The One*, for a work of its own, by chance in an insecure time.

The whole recovery was one big hill to climb, with many peaks along the way; summiting just to feel normal, and even great, for a little while.

First, I should mention that the toenail infection spread to the other foot. I went to another hospital in Boston after staying in the intensive care unit, and while I was there, I noticed that the big toenail on the other foot, my right foot, was beginning to yellow. Sometime later while recovering it yellowed. Four toes and both feet were infected, but the infection was not as concerning as the ordeal, the injuries, and the recovery needed my attention.

I was on crutches for a couple of months after getting discharged from the hospital and most of that time I stayed in bed, which was part of the recovery. It was the first phase of the recovery, in a way. My back hurt, and the only time that it did not was in bed. Part of the recovery, or at least the first part of it, was allowing things to heal. Then toward the end of that phase the pain went away, many of the fractures healed, and for the next phase I was cleared to walk, to start exercising, strengthening, but without exerting high-impact stress on my right leg because it was the right side of my pelvis that had been operated on. Then, the final phase of the recovery was essentially returning to normal, resuming all activities, low-impact and high-impact. It took about six months, and a lot of strength and suffering, to try and get back to the condition that I was in before. Some aspects of it seemed better, and some seemed worse.

During the first recovery phase, stuck in bed, many foods did not digest well. In the hospital, that system did not function properly, but it seemed better while recovering at the house, though some foods potentially made it worse; foods that were high in all kinds of sugars. But being bed-bound and quite uncomfortable, there was little else to remedy that feeling, at that house, in that condition, and those foods made me feel good—temporarily, while eating them. It did not take long though to put on some weight.

But I can still taste some of those deserts from the bakery, much later. They were delicious! Senses are memorable.

Around that time I was cleared from the crutches and started the second phase of the recovery. Also, I stepped on a scale and saw that I had gained some weight. The number was much greater than I expected, so I exercised a lot more to try and lose the extra weight. But it was really because being active at that time, strengthening the injuries, I felt very good. After being stuck in bed for three months and having almost a dormant digestive system, being active got things moving and like before it helped with the abdominal discomfort, which even in bed had been bad at times, from all the pain, the pain medications, and the foods that I consumed.

Most of the time I went for walks, in the morning, afternoon, or night, and other times I performed basic calisthenics. As long as the exercises were low-impact and caused little or no stress to my right leg, I was able to perform them. I felt better while I was performing them, and even afterward. But typically after eating, sometime after eating, the stomach pain returned.

Early in the summer I went to see an acupuncturist. It was for many different aches and pains, all still lingering from the ordeal, but I mainly went for the pains in my stomach, which had been persisting all along. The setting there was very relaxing. Little origami figures hung from the ceiling and twirled as calming music played softly from the walls. The acupuncturist poked needles into different extremities, usually my toes, the most vulnerable part of my body. I did not mention the yellow toenails, but I was vocal about the stomach pain. The acupuncturist knew that it was my main reason for going, and then I received herbs to help treat the issue because the acupuncture itself was not quite doing the trick, at that time.

The herbs might have helped in some way, but the discomfort always came back and almost always in the form of distension. So, I kept exercising, hiking, walking, and was soon cleared by the surgeon for high-impact activity, and then I really started running. Again, I felt great while running, and though great was only normal, it was much better than it had been.

There were several reasons why running during this time was so important. I ran on trails through the woods and always uphill, except for going down the hill. That signifies the recovery, everything, is just one big hill with ups and downs, but it was all this movement climbing up and down, joyously, that used much more energy than I consumed. I ate well, but how quickly the gained weight dropped. And don't forget, I was arrested before the ordeal took place, and all throughout the recovery the legal case was ongoing. I went through the usual procedures in court, had an arraignment, and then was due back in court at the end of that summer to have a hearing. It was a bit stressful, and the stress affected the abdominal discomfort, the distension. But running up and down the hills helped combat the cycle, as things went on, unusually.

It was a good time, just being able run and feel all right while running, after nearly not making it. Much more about that, the recovery, and the legal case is described in *The One*; to avoid being over repetitive in this book. I had a decent but definitely not a great outcome during the final court date at the end of that summer, just in time to resume college for the fall semester. I was guilty of trespassing in that store, and despite this as well as the discomfort, the distension, I truly felt good during this brief period, this transitional phase, and optimistic, like I was at the top of the hill.

Chapter 30

About a few weeks later I got dermatitis. I believe that it was related to the toenail infection, that the problem as a whole was internal. Then, because of the stress from all that had happened in the previous eight months, it got worse and spread to the opposite part of my body, the top of my head. The type of dermatitis was a kind of fungal infection, and it first caused inflammation and itching, and then the flakes came back. They were almost the same as they had been when I was a little kid—formed flakes, and slightly yellow, though not many. But this time there was inflammation and itching. Even at first it was bad, and along with the other discomforts, it was terrible.

One of the discomforts was new. I had not seen many people that I knew from before the ordeal after it happened, and when I did, it seemed much different. At least, it seemed like no one knew or cared about the suffering that I had been through, and then they also cold-shouldered me, which I thought was wrong. They thought or assumed something, and as the situation got worse, I understood it a little better. The dermatitis was definitely stressful at that time, but seemingly knowing their assumptions was just as stressful if not more, much more, and the stress altogether made the stomach discomfort even harder to bear.

Most food contributed to the problem as well, same reason as before, this and everything else. All the problems happened at once, only a few weeks into the semester. I changed conditions so drastically. The insecurities and these issues at that time have already been written about—including the assumptions and what made engineering so difficult—in *The*

One. My head reeled from all the problems. It was too much to deal with on top of everything else, and the coursework, so I withdrew from classes. It was a good decision. My body had not healed. And figuring that out, how to heal, was the priority.

Chapter 31

I left campus less than a month later. During that time the dermatitis got worse, and it continued to worsen at the house, as the seasons changed. The abdominal discomfort was strong, and a few weeks after leaving campus I saw a doctor about it. I had a procedure, an endoscopy, to try and detect any discernable problems, even cancer. I did not eat for probably twelve hours before the procedure, so there was very little discomfort going into it, since the discomfort occurred mainly after eating, and when they explored around my abdomen with an endoscope, a small camera on the end of a flexible medical tube, there was likely no irritation or inflammation. They said that they had found nothing wrong, or they assumed that since I was 20 there was nothing wrong and they did not thoroughly look for anything that might be wrong or think of any other conditions that it might be.

The dermatitis covered my scalp for a little while, and the inflammation and itching got more severe. I saw a doctor for it and received a few different forms of treatment, topical treatments, but they were not effective. For some people they might be, but the root of my problem was internal.

This period has sort of blurred over time. Part of the reason was because, understandably, I had trouble sleeping. Another part was because of all the stress, and lack of sleep caused stress, and stress made it hard to sleep, which also made the bigger problem worse, as well as the individual ones. A lot of pain. Yet I still went to school for that spring semester.

I should mention, I am making the problems during this time seem much less painful than they actually were. Each one that I mentioned was greatly amplified, and there were more that are unmentioned in this book, but are mentioned in the first book. There was anguish, and that is an insecurity. I had never experienced anything like it before. I had difficulty concentrating, functioning, forming associations. It was debilitating, and such a stressful time.

At college they enrolled me in a disability program, which I found hilarious. It was because of my traumatic brain injury, but I thought that the other problems were much more disabling, plaguing, and if anything, only these were affecting me then, and only the problems would affect my work. As far as I knew, my brain had healed one hundred and ten percent. While recovering, at times it seemed sharper than it ever had before. It had returned to normal even, while staying in the hospitals, less than a month after the ordeal itself. I was very lucid. But the problems, mainly the anguish that I had experienced, caused it to feel somewhat slow. I knew that it would not last forever, the unusual, painful feeling. I thought that it was only a low point, an abyss, which somehow I had to navigate out of. Something would bring about the transition. What, or how, I did not know yet.

I took the same classes as everyone else, but I had some additional resources that almost no one else had. I was allowed extra time to complete assignments, and if I asked for help, I could get it. People would essentially take notes for me on various subjects, but I still did my own work, of course. Much of it was writing, something, and one teacher even thought that it was exceptional. To write took some mental energy, and it was just the right amount to draw my attention away from all the problems, but not nearly enough to exacerbate any of them. Writing suddenly became very therapeutic, and unknowingly it led to the transition.

For the semester, I had transferred to a different school, one that was pretty close to the house in which I grew up, and I took classes there until I received the required credits and graduated, but I was only at that house for that first semester.

The problems continued while I was there, but I found some remedies for at least one of them, shampoo and a certain oil that alleviated the dermatitis, which reduced stress, relieving some of the other discomforts. These were not cures, especially for the bigger internal problem, but in part they helped me out of the low point that year, and the rest was writing.

Usually, while I was at that house, I spent my time down in the basement. That was probably the only space in that house where I could work, think, write, dream. I remembered early on that, before the ordeal, I had the idea of writing a book, and my idea of writing a book then had changed a lot after the start of the ordeal. Or at least my idea of what the book would be about had changed, because I had changed, after it happened. Before the ordeal I had the idea of writing a book, and also that it might be about what *Any Moment* is based on, but I was still unsure at that time; unsure if I would even try to write the book. Then the ordeal happened and I was at a crossroads, and because I did not get closure, because it was all endured, I absolutely had something to write about. The idea of writing a book about it became my notion of getting closure, and I still think that it was a good way to respond to the adversity, rather than giving up.

So, the idea of writing my first book about the ordeal and its aftermath was established, or cemented, in that basement. The house had three floors and the basement was unfinished, all concrete, or cement. I tried starting the book in the basement, but it was unlike any other written work that I had done before. To write something big that takes more than one sitting, something that takes multiple sittings in the same spot, the space and environment should be good. Many places work, but for that task, that house was not one of them. Many ideas sprouted down there, but for them to flourish, and to bring the project to fruition, I had to get out of that house. Late spring I moved into an apartment, and then I really started working on the idea.

Chapter 32

I remember it being sultry that summer in the fifth floor apartment. There were high ceilings and big windows with a lot of sunlight, but, no air conditioner. Next summer there was, but that year it was sultry and I sweat. I may have already written in a different book that I had heard more energy is used by the brain during brain work than the body during exercise, like writing vs running. It was a good summer. I wrote a lot, the first draft of the first book, and I ran a lot, exercised, and did a lot. Hence, I burned calories, sweat, and the dermatitis persisted on and off.

The space and the environment were great for learning how to take on a big project, which I had never done before and had probably never been done before as a means of getting closure. And, there was probably nothing else like it that had been done before in that place; what a climax! The apartment building was in a good spot downtown, a quick walk to the waterfront and the store, and all around were restaurants and bars, also craft beer. I had turned 21 earlier that winter, and if I wanted to enjoy a beer in different settings, there were many places close by to go to, just steps from the building.

During the summer, I noticed that this beverage, in moderation, had almost a therapeutic effect on the abdominal discomfort. It somehow relieved the distension, and though the beverage itself did not exactly help with writing, the relief that it produced made it easier to write in every respect. They were still there in my stomach, the discomfort and distension, just less noticeable. Whereas other times it was much more intense, and obviously, distracting. Writing or any other work or art takes concentration, and most of the time that was how I wrote the first draft, through the discomfort and distension, using more energy to try and get it done than on the occasions when it felt normal. But every now and then, on occasion, it was good to get some relief and feel, better. It was not that while having a beer I took a break; the ideas were constantly ruminating, and I had to figure how to get them down somehow. Water was the only other beverage that seemed to sit well, but it was neutral, it did not cause discomfort or provide relief. Milk and fruit juices were usually problematic, and a lot of other beverages were too. It was hard to figure out which ones were all right and which ones caused problems. As far as beverage options went.

My mind had been in a funk, and it had experienced serious anguish after the ordeal and then throughout the aftermath of it. The new apartment, that unique space which was "mine" while I inhabited it, was exactly what I needed to get better. That, getting better, might have just been getting back to "normal," but now that I was working on and toward something, normal was not even an option. The past year that I was writing about was not normal, and I expected others to study it, change perspectives because of it, which was not normal, but at times in that past year I had felt almost subnormal, so while doing that, while doing it, I felt great... aside from the discomforts.

Working through the dermatitis and distension was just inefficient. It seemed almost like I had to use twice as much energy to do the same amount of work, if things were normal. And even though things became better after finding some temporary remedies, when the discomforts came back, externally they were still somewhat noticeable. But, because the root cause was internal, they always came back and they were always somewhat noticeable. This was mostly true for the dermatitis, which not only I noticed, its pinkish color, but maybe others did too.

I went to a barber shop nearby for haircuts. It was only a short walk away on the other side of the hill, and inside there were couches, recliners, TVs, a whole lounge area to wait in before getting a trim. The same girl cut my hair every time, and she seemed to like grooming me. She sometimes parted my hair and thoughtfully examined my scalp, but for all I know, she was unable to tell if something was wrong, or if she could help. There definitely was, and if she had, that would have been appreciated.

I had a hard time shaping the idea of a book into book form. It was the first time that I had done something like it, and after multiple books it is still hard to do, but instead of stressing over its structure like I did then, I now see its completed form as a kind of art, with or without a particular structure.

When I had difficulty with something, trying to figure out one aspect of the book or another, or if the discomforts were hard to bear and they were too much to work through, I went for a run, felt relieved, and usually found the answer. I ran on a trail through the woods that followed a river, and there were many hills and different kinds of terrain, which made or inspired some good ideas. If something was difficult and I went for a run, usually while going along the river or after making it to the top of a hill, an idea to get past the difficulty came to mind and I wrote it down, then added it to the book afterward—or the structure, of the book.

Many ideas came to mind while exercising. Somehow that has always been a fairly certain way to get inspired. But I did not always write something down, and it was the best ideas that stayed to see the page. A great writer said that he does not write down ideas; the mind is like a sieve, and most ideas will sift through the sieve while the best ideas stay in the sieve, then see the page.

There was another benefit to this, going for a run, and it was the same as it had been before and after the ordeal. My abdomen felt better while running along the trail than it did while say sitting, like exercising, but running the trail was a thrill, and after running or exercising it continued to feel all right, even good, even while sitting in one place, until consuming something upset my inner world. It was one of the only times that my stomach felt good, while running, exercising, sometimes rubbing it. And there was another benefit too. After going back to the apartment, my scalp felt better while showering, and it felt good until the next big sweat, causing a flare-up.

It took a while to finish the first draft, and it was interesting to sift through the past and relive the moment later; interesting, but exhausting even, the first time, the first draft of the first book. And then to make a whole manuscript, study it and see its structure, that was good too.

I had a timer going and the amount of time that was left was displayed right below the clock on my phone, and the first time that I checked to see how much time was left on the timer, it was exactly the same time as the time on the clock, 8:44, but the timer below went to 8:43, 8:42, 8:41, and it took me until then to realize that that was the timer, not the actual clock, and that time was not going backwards. I was puzzled for a few seconds, then realized, some writing is timeless.

Chapter 33

One time during the following year I buzzed my hair. It was definitely a buzz cut, and even though it was buzzed for only a little while, it felt good. The damages from that past year were easy to perceive, more so on the inside, but also from the outside. In fact, that was why I did it in the first place. Winter was bad for the dermatitis. It seemed like that condition responded poorly to certain climates and climate changes, the weather and the changing seasons, heaters and heating systems. The barber noticed that my scalp seemed slightly inflamed, as if it had to do with my immune system, if it was an immune response. I went to a different barber, and he said, "Try getting under some UV light. It helps a lot with it. See?"

"Okay," I said. "Violet light. Interesting."

He held a mirror behind my head. It was buzzed. There was some redness, and that part was itchy. Just seeing it seemed to bring about that sensation. I noticed the scar from the ordeal on the back of my head, shaped like an X. It was the first time I had seen it, and it all felt good, then even better after leaving, when a soft breeze swept through.

That fall had been a busy time of year, working on the book and taking classes. Not long after the start of that season there was more anguish, which might have been why the discomforts were worse later that winter, and it was right around that time when the trail that I ran on became covered in leaves basically overnight and I had to stop. I ran on a treadmill inside and it was just not the same.

Maybe this was partly why the stress came back. But I think that it was mostly because I had worked very hard over the summer, and in a way, over the following months, I saw almost no light at the end of the tunnel with the book, because it was my first book, and because I had great expectations of it but not a clue of how to get it to them. It seemed as though I was traumatized from such a bizarre, unusually distressing past, and it's hard to admit that it is an insecurity. Being a victim and survivor of something, some kind of foul play, and many more problems and circumstances before the ordeal, it is almost embarrassing to write that, much more than maybe anything else. All of that is part of myself, much more so, perhaps, than anything else, because it is those insecurities, everything that happened while growing up, that have shaped my perspective into something, worth writing, or what brings worth to the writing. It was hard writing at first, after everything, but I found it, and I had not found anything else. Then later I really enjoyed it, maybe loved it, and I still do. I am just glad that I did not give up, I think, and I almost did, because that would have been easy to do, but I was only going through another transitional phase, battling the past, all at once, hard, hard, hard to do, then maybe great.

At least it was a good feeling finishing the second draft of that first book, writing it, that is, and it happened just in time for the presentation. I had never been much of a public speaker, and after going through that angst, battling anguish, and writing so much, I went up and gave a fine presentation—impromptu. As long as I have something to start with, some subject, matter, problem, or idea to discuss, maybe, it will be at least somewhat interesting. Some people have something to say about anything, or everything. What the topic was that day I do not remember very well. Just about every day there was a new topic, and same with many since then. I had no preparation or notes, but I felt good. The nerves were gone, and I didn't notice any discomforts. Soon the presentation tapered off.

I was asked some questions regarding the topic.

Then, maybe answered, "That is not enough these days."

Chapter 34

Shortly after the new year I finished editing the manuscript. It had about 30,000 more words than the first draft, and back then I thought that it was much better than that draft. It was, and I was thrilled to finish it. I printed out the full manuscript on 8.5x11 inch computer paper, then fit it into a manilla envelope, and sent it to someone who I admired greatly. He had helped me through some difficult times, or at least his work had, and I hoped to catch his attention, then hear back from him. Knowing my past, all that was unsaid about life before the ordeal in the first book, I did not expect much except potentially, somehow, a good word to a publisher, or even from him, but I figured, I'd probably endure everything, a little more, a bit heavier, it's just the first book, just don't give up. And that is in a way what happened. I didn't give up, but I never heard back, then. I knew that soon the weather would change for the better, in my opinion, and before long some discomforts would also get better.

Springtime was very busy that year. I was hardly at the apartment, but I was always working on the book somewhere. I worked on it even at work. Most people there did whatever pleased them on the computers or their laptops, including the boss. I plugged away on the book or else completed assignments, tasks, and other duties. The boss was kind, but sometimes I got a hard time because of the arrest that had occurred a week before the ordeal, because that event was on my record, and the boss saw it. But it only showed the surface of the event, the charges, the date, the dismissal, the unconditional discharge, but nothing else to it, which I made sure to include in the first book.

One of my expectations for the first book was publishing it traditionally, and the other expectation, following the first one, was starting a literary career. The expectation was for that to happen before graduating from university, because there, my observations were not quite aligned with my perspective. It was ambitious; some chance and luck and kindness I would need! I sent query letters for that first book to many agents and publishers, and of course I mentioned that I planned to write more books. The past went deep, several books deep.

The plan was to continue with it, because I had found it and after struggling with it at first, because of everything, I then enjoyed it, as a coping mechanism for everything. Even just the thought of doing it for the long haul, that made some of the pain more endurable. It was then that the discomforts, though they were still there, seemed to evaporate, like the insecurities. It was then that things felt all right.

But, I never heard back from really any people in the literary industry. From all those query letters, and after all that time spent writing them, then waiting, I vividly remember only one of the few responses. I was congratulated for being a survivor. Simply, congratulations for being a survivor. That was about it. I nearly teared-up, that one stung.

I wondered, wouldn't they care to help someone who has had a very painful past, and wouldn't it be right to help them out, or essentially pick them up, early? (Instead of just letting someone endure all that pain, everything coming back, all at once, several times, in waves, a feeling that I would only tell, maybe, one person, because it's heavy and now an insecurity. All pain all feelings everything is perceived in the mind. Almost all the physical pain I'd experienced up to that point, maybe several months after the big event, when the first wave crashed, was eased with pain medication as soon as I had it. The medications, their active ingredients, bind to receptors in the central nervous system, the gut and other parts of the body, decreasing the feeling of pain, and increasing the tolerance to pain. It's like the gut-brain connection. But I had no pain medication, and no one cared, as all the pain endured throughout life came back at once, and even though what all that pain had manifested into was not actually happening, it felt like it was. It took getting an all-day tattoo cover up and not really feeling anything to realize what the feeling that came in waves must be like, incredible pain, after a few waves, and it all lasted much longer than a day. A few years earlier was when I was waiting after submitting all those queries for the very first book.) This was when I only understood the discomforts superficially, like how they felt and affected everything, but now that I understand them, especially what causes them, I still would be, but even more so.

Chapter 35

A goal that I had after first starting the book was getting it published before the day that I would have graduated from college if the ordeal had not happened. The expectation was to publish it traditionally; the goal was to publish it before the original or former graduation date. After waiting long enough and realizing that to reach the goal there was not a lot of time in that frame, I really got going on it. The trees just started to blossom, it was that time of year, and on the sidewalk below my apartment window were a few flowering trees and they were good omens.

I had three days off, and for those three days I wrote and edited the book almost nonstop. Three days can easily turn to three weeks, plus, what concentration. It got a bit tiring toward the end. Then, I could think like a student, from that perspective, and I hadn't realized that say, a painter, might not spend time editing his or her painting, but what I was trying to do with the book was almost like a painting, autobiographical surrealism.

What would happen if *The Stolen Mirror* was edited? It would no longer be the artist, the painter. And why would the painter, the artist, make a description for their painting, that surreal world?

In any case, the goal was met, and that book was published just about a week before the graduation date. I was supposed to graduate that year in May, if the ordeal had not happened, and after writing about it a few times in less than a year, the book finally came out on the last day of April. I published it myself, and though meeting the goal felt great, and having a book under my belt felt even better, it seemed much less, fulfilling, notable, than it could have been... if I had gotten some help from the literary industry, possibly even figures like gods. I was pleased with it, but not fully.

On the date that it was published I also had a presentation, and I mainly talked about the book, how it took a lot of strength to finish creating it, and how the goal was met.

Someone asked, "Do you have any events lined up, any book talks?"

"Not yet," I said—smiling.

"What's next?"

"Another chapter, perhaps."

The next week I caught a bad bug. It was some kind of viral infection, though it could have been bacterial, and I was very sick for a little while. The problem probably had to do with having a weakened immune system, at least from all the work and hurt over the past, long while. It felt worse than the flu, but it was not as bad or strange as some infections before then. Oh, but I did it. I had the book in my hand before I would have graduated in that other world, ceased just over a year earlier, or even as early as the start of the first world. I still had the discomforts to deal with, and they were the same as they always had been, flaring up from time to time but always having at least a slight presence.

Then, another chapter started. The book was published on the last day of April, but that book, the first one, is no longer in print. After about two months, that first book almost became an insecurity, because my writing was not as developed as it is now, but the knowledge was there, and the intelligence. I was not used to the fact that, this just builds layers. It happened sometime after returning from New York. I had gone there to try and potentially get it acquired by a traditional publisher, but it did not happen that time. I returned somewhat unhappy, not so much from the shortcomings, but just with the book itself, and even everything else. Maybe too much angst and anguish that was experienced while writing it showed. Then I started rewriting it, and a few weeks later, I took that first book out of print.

It was the same storyline, and I thought that the rewrite would not take long, but it took about four months to finish. I was a full-time student, and most weeks I also worked full time, but if not, close to it. So I worked on the book during any spare time that I had, and it probably added up to well over 40 hours a week, just rewriting and editing, for some reason. For a little while, the discomforts were less noticeable than they had been, and it might have been the busy schedule that sort of dulled them, whereas it was usually the discomforts that made everything else worse. It lasted for a couple of weeks, this sense of ease, and I enjoyed it.

Much of the work for that book, the rewrite, was done in November and December. I got carried away rewriting and editing it, probably from spending so much time on that part of it. Then sometime around late December or early January the book was published. The goal was to finish it by Christmas, and though the publication date may have been on Christmas day or the day after, I did not finish editing it until about a week later. Those additional changes were reflected in printed and digital copies, but I was overworked and unsatisfied while rewriting it, and I thought that that was what really showed. I was pleased with it at first, of course, but somewhat quickly that feeling fleeted. Maybe the misfortune, the ordeal, the event on which that book is based, was also becoming an insecurity, sad as that might be. Well, that book stayed in print for less time than the first one, and I took it out of print for almost the same reason as the first one, then realized, there was still time for another one.

Chapter 36

I planned to graduate after the first summer term, and then after graduating, move to San Diego. Two of my cousins lived in Southern California. They had moved there at least a few years earlier, and in a way, that almost inspired me to as well. After the whole ordeal, the tough recovery, all the writing, the work, the shortcomings, I had a great urge for an adventure and also good weather. Plus, after the ordeal, everyone I knew and had grown up with made everything else worse, and I felt very low. I had no one for some time, at that house, where I was. But in San Diego there were more people, and maybe some of them would feel for me and my story, where I was coming from. Not where I was raised, but the pain.

Before moving, I tried hard to get the book right. I had gotten much better at writing since finishing the first book the first time, and I thought that getting it right would make all the difference in the world, but I did not realize that the internal problem would have much more of an impact on that than the book. Yet, I knew that I had to get in better shape, that would help with the problem, and potentially with the book. So, there was a lot to do in not a lot of time.

Then suddenly, everyone was ordered to stay inside. There was a virus spreading rapidly and knowing my immune system, its troubles in the past, I just did not want to get sick again, and I really enjoyed all the time inside. In the past, while writing and rewriting the first book, I got antsy sometimes if it seemed nice outside. But for the third and final rewrite, there was a good reason to stay inside, and it gave me much more time to try and get it right. Also, I was much more focused on trying to improve the internal problem. I was getting myself in good health, then feeling good.

Little by little, or perhaps day by day, what I was doing began to ease the discomforts. My stomach felt better, although it did not feel great, but it was better than normal just by eating more mindfully. Certain foods still caused some kind of reaction, of course, and I could never quite figure out which ones were good to eat and which ones were problematic, but during that time things did feel better. And, not that it was even a problem, but how the weight dropped!

That was just one thing, eating more mindfully. Another thing that I did, which definitely burned calories and eased the discomforts, was exercise more intensely and regularly than I had before. I had a routine that I did inside, and then at night, I went for long runs through downtown and to both promenades. During the day I might have seen a few people walking outside or a car driving by, at the start of the pandemic, but running through the streets at night, there was no one. It was strange, but awesome. No other experience compared, and all around the world at that time it was the same, but I must have been one of the only ones doing it. Ah, running. I had been too busy to run or even full-on workout earlier that fall, but that spring, with all the extra time, I did both, and I began to feel great, at least for half of the day. I ran always at night, so if I ate beforehand and felt any discomfort, which almost always happened, running after would ease the discomfort just as it always had, and as long as I ate nothing else after, that good feeling would last at least until the morning.

Every day I did something, calisthenics of sorts inside, and running outside. They were very effective against the stomach discomfort and any other kind of affliction.

Also, the dermatitis seemed to be getting better, and one reason was because the seasons were changing, winter to spring and then spring to summer. Being inside or outside had

113

almost no noticeable effect on the condition. It was always there, and it was better when I felt better.

But there was another reason why it seemed to be improving, and it had to do with the internal problem. In part, the yellow toenail. I had moved into the apartment with four of them, four yellow toenails, and by the time that the pandemic broke out, that infection had spread to all but three toenails. It was clearly an insecurity, and in a way, it was also concerning... I not only wanted to feel good in San Diego, but I also wanted to look good wearing sandals. So, around the time that the stay-at-home orders were put into effect, I went to see a doctor about the yellow toenails and was prescribed an antifungal medication. It was probably the same one that I had taken as a kid, the name of it sounded familiar, and its effects, the results, were very similar. After about a month of taking the medication daily, my toenails started growing out normally; from the inside, wherever nails grow out from. Then after three months, they mostly cleared up. It was not long after I had started taking the medication that the dermatitis seemed to be getting at least a little better, but that was also right around the time that the seasons changed. The weather was warmer, better. Perhaps both had a positive effect.

Anyway, I picked up another three-month supply of that medication after it ran out, and I continued taking it to prevent the infection from returning to my toenails, just as it had when I was a kid as soon as I stopped taking it.

I did not consume anything that I thought might cause a reaction with that antifungal medication. I really only had water to drink and a few different foods to eat, and I ran or exercised so much that I only faintly noticed the discomfort that these foods caused. Well, there were eggs, avocados, guacamole, chicken, tacos, sauces, and a lot of ingredients in those sauces... But overall, I felt better during that time than any other period before then, had more energy, clarity, enthusiasm, drive. It seemed like things would only continue to get better internally.

I believe that the third rewrite was my best effort given the circumstances, at least for that book, my first book. It took three or four months to finish it, just because to graduate after the first term that summer, I had to take nearly two terms of classes in one. Even then, I was still, exactly, one credit shy from meeting the graduation requirements. I had 119 credits and needed 120. I argued with them that I wrote two books and was working on a third while being enrolled, and professors had even borrowed some of my ideas from the book and reiterated them in class without giving credit, so I thought that it only seemed fair to waive the one credit that I needed considering the circumstance: I was the exception to the rule. But, for some reason, I still had to do it, a lot of extra work to get that one credit. I had to basically explain what the book inspired, in a long paper that was part of a portfolio, and the entire time I was painfully laughing, like crying, as what the book had actually inspired was happening all around the world at that time. Of course I did not mention that in the paper. But aw, it still pains me; I could not catch a break with anything. It was hard to get everything done and then finish the book before moving to San Diego, considering everything, but I did it.

On the day that I had the book in my hands, I went on one last run along the trail that followed the river, and there have been many other runs since then, but that one is different. I imagined, like those in Big Sur... It was a miniature wilderness, running along the river and up the hill, down the valley and under the trees, and I thought about how great it was in the rising light.

I remembered the struggles in the book, the pains, the time that won't come back, that should be worth a lot. Then there were all the people, places, good moments, bad moments, but not once thinking about the discomforts, everything from the past; it was all too hard to imagine then. I was running, eager. The trail kept going, the water was flowing, in and along the river. I spent the night packing, then in the morning, set off on the road to San Diego.

Chapter 37

This book is not rushed. Much of this period and some of the experiences have already been described in a different book, and I'm trying not to sound repetitive. But maybe one day all of these books, four in total so far, will be offered as a package, considered a quartet, if there are publishers out there who can help.

The road trip to San Diego was somewhat uneventful. I stopped for the night in Cleveland, Des Moines, Denver, Moab, Las Vegas, and they were all unique, the experiences, the roads, all different. There was the sunset at Lake Eerie, and there were acres and acres of fields, a big elevation gain, and then the plains. The Rocky Mountains were big, surrounded by miles of blue, and somewhere ahead the sunrise commenced. Then appeared canyons, and out there sat the Delicate Arch, the Double Arch, the Balanced Rock. The landscape went from alpine to desert in just over a day, and then the next one, the next day, there was the smell of salt in the air, coastal fog, a cool ocean breeze. I arrived, in Pacific Beach.

San Diego was nice. I was very busy, and I went all around the city and every neighborhood working on the road, the entire time, taking notes for a future book that later I wrote in Los Angeles.

That started shortly after arriving, working on the road as a contractor, seeing and understanding the city, and there were many experiences all throughout the adventure. These are part of the period that I was talking about, they're in a different book. So, I saw the city, though I did not quite *experience* it. Venues were closed and for much of the time restaurants offered takeout only. I saw the land and the various landscapes, canyons, hills, mountains, beaches, but not quite the city's, and each neighborhood's, unique nightlife. This is a big part of the whole picture—of any city. Day and night is only half of the picture; the experience day and night is the other half of the picture.

In that case, I did not experience the full picture of any city on the road to San Diego. It was an unusual long-distance road trip. There was always a slight worry that something bad might happen to the car, and then some kind of misfortune would occur. It was a bit tiring, so every city that I stopped in, I just explored the city and then went back to the hotel. After arriving in San Diego, I regretted not quite experiencing those cities full on. Granted, most establishments all around the world at that time were either temporarily closed or had capacity restrictions. I figured that, next time I would.

Although I did not rightly experience this aspect of the city, the nightlife in San Diego, I was often on the road there and I did get to taste it—another important aspect of every city, its food, but it can sometimes be hard on the digestive system. I ate all around the city and in almost every neighborhood, delicious tacos, burritos, many, sauces, vegetables, seasonings, spices...

The discomforts were there, definitely noticeable, but while being on the road, taking notes, they were almost less noticeable because these things were comforting. And the other problems seemed to be, in a way, pacific, as though the ocean itself, that half of creation, pacified them.

Even though the dermatitis was still somewhat noticeable, but only to me, how it felt, it was less inflamed, itchy, and discomforting than it had been in the past, like earlier that winter. But it was summer and even a different climate; they both felt good.

I still took that medication, and my toes were all right. I only wore sandals, except for those nights that I went on a run. Running was still therapeutic, and because it was night, also wonderful. The routes varied from time to time, but what

117

really varied were the sights on the route, all around Crown Point. Some nights in the park there were performers, dancers, artists, campers, or campfires, and I noticed that after a little while more people started running at night as well, sometimes when I was heading out, or going back to the condo, where I lived, on Hornblend.

It was a good room on the top floor, centrally located. Nearby were several shopping centers, strip malls, restaurants, bars. The latter two I would have just loved to experience, but I was busy, and most of those places were temporarily closed.

My cousins lived about an hour or two away, one county north, and also in the eastern part of the county. We all got together one weekend, out east, where it was mountainous and rural. I picked up a few pies along the way and someone else got food and drinks. It was enough for at least a few days.

After arriving, I experienced an unusual kind of, revelation, or insight, in a way, and it had also happened in the Grand Canyon, Great Lakes, Rocky Mountains, and many other places before and after; feeling like I had been there before, like I knew the land completely, as though I had seen and even explored it before, in a past life, past time, before time. It might have just been the desert, the mirage in the valley, or a kind of past-life experience, creating this evocative feeling.

At some point after lunch or dinner, or after breakfast the next day, that special feeling went away, and there might have been a reason why. I had never had so much pie at once, and my stomach felt very distended, sour even, but the pies were delicious. It reduced the evocative feeling that I had at first, and I no longer thought about what it might have been, could be, or what it meant. I had mostly avoided eating sugar for several months, and then suddenly I had many different sugars at once. Pie was really all that I had to eat for a couple of days, and I definitely did not feel very good after returning to the city. Even taking notes and being on the road, then running around the neighborhood at night, hardly eased the discomfort for a little while. At least, that was the case after the second time that I went out east in the county. I was not yet on the road after the first time, but the feeling was the same, not great.

Later that month I went to Los Angeles to do what I did in New York with the first book. Only this time it was with the final rewrite of the first book that I had just finished. I stopped at a few places around the city, starting in downtown, and from there going west, but I did not even get a glimpse of it. Perhaps, what came close to it later was the view of the city to the south and to the west from my spot in the hills. It was there that I noted how vast and advanced the area seemed, and that was only one part of it. There was also the valley to the north, which that time I did not get to see or experience. It was inspiring though, to think about how it all might operate, a mega city, so intricately. This is true for a lot of cities. And I sought to be part of it.

When I was going around with the book, I talked to people at only a few places. They were maybe boutique agencies, and even though, briefly, I talked with at least one woman in the literary industry, and I was hopeful afterward, I did not come away with representation that time. But, sometime later when I did learn about that, I was in San Diego.

There I continued on the road and took notes for another month and a half. I drove a lot, on many different roads, paved and unpaved and for some, getting paved, and the entire time The Honda ran smoothly. There were no problems with it, and aside from the internal problems, the discomforts, pains that those problems caused, and other events causing those, there were not many problems with anything else, except that I felt so close to something I could not rest so easily. Then, my urge to continue writing and to try and foster a literary career brought me back to Los Angeles, and a new home.

Chapter 38

The apartment building where I lived was nearly on the line between Hollywood and the Hollywood Hills. It was technically in the latter of those two neighborhoods, and that was where I wrote the next two books after *The One*. After the first one there, I started writing the second one with the idea that all three could be considered a trilogy. They are all interrelated, the first three books, and in a way, this fourth book almost ties them together, but not quite. That's because after finishing the third one, *Any Moment*, I thought that there was an essential component missing to all three: the insecurities. They had been unpleasant in the past, and they are very much part of the past, those storylines. Then they got even worse for some time while living in Los Angeles, it was almost like an ordeal, and because of that, those two books were hard to write. It will be easy to understand why in this book, especially after starting the second book there. What an unexpected event!

That happened six months after moving in, and some things happened before then, even right away. First, I should mention that I stopped taking the fungal medication as soon as I moved in. I had been on it for several months, and since it seemingly made the abdominal discomfort worse, apparently by affecting the microbiome inside me and the balance of internal microbiota, stopping it seemed smart. And it was. But it took a lot of strength to essentially try and repair or reset the microbiome, later.

After discontinuing the medication, I knew how my toenails would eventually look, and I thought that it was worth it. Plus, I wore shoes more often. But how soon the infection came back!

Also, I must mention that I was in shape on the day that I moved in. But there were some minor complications upon moving in... I forgot that I had to schedule an appointment with the Los Angeles Department of Water and Power, before moving in, to actually have power upon moving in, and I moved in on a Friday, but they were unable to turn on the power in the apartment that day, and they were closed for the weekend, a long weekend, so I stayed with my cousin over the weekend until my apartment had power, the following week. There I ate somewhat poorly, if at all, and though I could have gone hiking, I did not exercise. This little excursion must have disrupted or changed something, at least the routine that I had, because when I went back to my apartment, it was very hard to get back into the, or even a, routine. A week went by without much exercise, other than walking through the neighborhood, and I almost got out of shape. Motivation was low, for a little while after, and it was much harder to get back into shape than it was to just maintain it, as I had been doing all along, and that did not even happen until after finishing the first book—at the new apartment.

In San Diego, I ran about four days a week, and some days I even went to the gym, but after moving to Los Angeles, I had a hard time getting myself to even go on a run, let alone to the gym. Motivation was low in that regard, yes, but I was also engrossed in creating the next book, after thinking about it, and then eventually starting it. At that time, I did not feel great because of the discomforts, which hindered my motivation, and also, at first, the neighborhood seemed, somewhat difficult, to run through at night. Almost every block there was a busy street that would have to be crossed, and many sidewalks all throughout were crowded. But later I found some spots nearby that turned out to be awesome for running, especially at night.

121

Since that did not happen until after finishing the first book there, while writing it, the discomforts seemed much more pronounced, and I felt worse than normal. Oh, they were quite noticeable! The dermatitis came back, badly. And sometimes while writing, the stomach discomfort was just too much to work through and I had to stop, nothing eased it. That was frustrating, and although the effect that it caused was similar to experiencing writer's block, it was worse because it was much more than that. It not only slowed down creativity, as though experiencing writer's block, but it also altered cognitive activity and it kind of hurt. I have a hard time describing what it felt like, a distended, sour ache, especially on the left side, but please understand that it was very distracting.

Not being in shape also affected the work, though not necessarily the output. Exercise clears and, defogs, the mind when there are discomforts, but I did not have a solid routine while writing that book, *Like That Star*. Yet I finished it in about three weeks. I had the notes from San Diego and some experiences dating back to the very first book, which definitely helped. I wrote it in a stream-of-consciousness fashion, and some of the frustrations that I mentioned earlier, like the discomforts and their effects, the pain, might have showed in the writing. They were definitely part of the picture at that time; I was just trying to write the book as fast as possible. It was all in the pursuit of expression, that kind of art, one style of writing compared to another, painting, but a novel.

One reason that the discomforts were more pronounced during that time was because I never knew what to eat, or rather which foods caused the discomforts. For all I knew, they all did. Or, it could have been that when some were consumed, only these caused the discomfort, and after consuming them, the discomfort lasted long enough to still be noticeable by the time that something else, causing discomfort, was consumed.

It was almost a science, just thinking about it, trying to grasp it, and it was hard enough as it was to articulate thoughts from the past in the present, in a stream-of-consciousness fashion. Then, to finish writing the book in as quickly as a few weeks, it was incredible, and felt great!

Then, all of a sudden, I had more time and energy to try and better understand the discomforts, what causes them, and to get back into shape.

I started with the latter almost immediately because exercise had always eased the discomforts. I was almost nervous to go on the first run, but afterward I was much more assured. I was even so pleased with it that I developed a routine and went on the same run every other day.

After working hard on the book, it was needed. Like, "Much obliged!"

For this routine, I always ran at night, through, or rather around, the historic Whitley Heights neighborhood! It was part of the original Hollywood Hills, and I lived at the base. The run itself was straightforward—going up Grace, then looping around the Terrace and and Place—but there were all sorts of turns, hills, dips, and cracks in the pavement which made the run a thrill. Running up Grace was a good warm up, and I always went at night, normally between 9:00pm and 12:00pm. The first time that I went I was the only one out, but almost every other time afterward, I saw people walking, and eventually, some people started running. Maybe they thought that I was getting in shape for a movie. Maybe I was. Maybe I just felt good. Some of the properties were like castles. It was fascinating, exciting. I never thought that I would run through that part of history, but I did, and I liked it. Up until then, they were the best runs that I had gone on.

One time there was a girl skateboarding—just on a section of flat ground, between all the cracks and dips in the pavement. I cupped my hands around my mouth and said, "Kickflip!" She laughed and got off the board.

"I can't!"

"Same."

123

"Try one," she said.

I did, landed, then ran on… Not! I did not land, but laughed, and then I ran on…

I kept the same routine of running around Whitley Heights for a while, even after starting the next book, *Any Moment*. There was not a lot of time between finishing *That Star* and starting *Any Moment*.

On top of continuing the routine and feeling better than normal, I made some dietary changes, which eventually led to lifestyle changes. I figured that the yellow toenails and the dermatitis were somehow related, that they were due to an internal infection, an imbalance of microbiota, bad bacteria, pathogens, fungi, and then I learned that sugars and starches were potentially feeding the fungi, and anything that turned to sugar in the digestive tract was fueling their activity, causing inflammation. So, I stopped eating sugar, and anything that turns to sugar after being broken down digestively. Then, I soon began noticing the positive effects; and even more so after starting a cleanse, which was part of the lifestyle change. The abdominal discomfort was still there, but it was much more bearable, and less distracting, discouraging.

After starting the next book, *Any Moment*, it was a lot easier and more enjoyable to write than the previous book. The idea of it actually came to mind while going on a run through the neighborhood, starting at the beginning, finishing at the end. That right there, the latter part of that idea, to my knowledge, had never been done before—autobiographically. Everything in between, in memory, seemed unique enough for a good book.

So, I was eager to start it, and I worked through it quickly, striving to write a, good book. Things were going well for a, little while. Then this, different, story happened.

Chapter 39

I had only just begun the cleanse, diet, lifestyle change when a woman living right across the hall asked me if I took her table. What she was referring to was kind of funny. It was much smaller than a coffee table, but it was still a table, and she had it out in the hall so delivery drivers could put her food and packages on something. I had seen it every time that I went into and left my apartment. She even had a note on her door letting couriers know to put her deliveries on the little table. But I did not take it. I didn't need a delivery table inside the apartment, and I liked to keep it, somewhat, uncluttered. I told her so. Then she said that it must have been someone else. Obviously, I thought. And then she went on to say that the building was caving in; changed subjects, that quickly. She was an unusual woman. Something was just not right. She was talking very fast, very unconventionally, in a way. But I was used to it from the issues with my brother. Nothing could top that. She pulled me aside.

"See this," she said. It was just a normal hallway wall. "Oh, and I don't even have hot water. Been here since Bush. No, hot, water!"

"What about your table?" I asked.

Her eyes enlarged. "Idon'tknow—" shaking her head, she said that at once.

I thought that it was funny, that our conversation was amusing. I had been interrupted from some deep thoughts, and I did not mind, it was a good break. Plus, it seemed like something was bound to happen, and that was exciting. I went back to the apartment.

About a week went by. I stayed very busy. I was writing ten hours a day. Think about the other fourteen. The book would not finish itself. I really enjoyed it, working on a big project like that. To me, in a way, as I've implied before, it was like working on a painting, just autobiographical. Anyway, about a week later her table was still gone. Then the next day when I left my apartment it was there, the same one as before, or the same kind of table at least. It was sometime in the morning and many people were at home, corona virus cases had recently spiked, numbers were always high, I was just going to get coffee. And there was the lady, talking to a girl down the hall. I was going to walk by. Then she stopped me. She said that they were just talking. Apparently, about ghosts. But really, it was just the woman talking, and it was in a peculiar way. I looked at the girl, caught a sidelong grin.

The following day, sometime around 9:00am, the lady came to my apartment and told me about, some strange things. We were standing right in my doorway, and I cannot explain what these things were, they were just highly out-there, but it all had something to do with ghosts and radiation and orbs of light and not having hot water. It reminded me again of my youth, my brother. But this time it was amusing. She probably just needed someone to, talk to. Then she showed me a video of one of the "orbs" in the dark, but to me it looked just like a cable modem light, blinking, and green. To her they were ghosts, radiation, and these were after her.

"I didn't mean to scare you," she said, in that peculiar way.

"Oh, that's all right," I said.

"Did the girl text you?"

"Yeah. How—"

"I think she likes you. I showed her the video too. Then—" she glanced down the hall quickly, looked back. "Okay, these walls have crawl spaces. Shh, hear that? There are people crawling between the walls."

I didn't say anything.

"We heard them yesterday, in the girl's apartment, shuffling around between the pipes. I think she's pretty, well, excited. I didn't mean to—shh, shh. Oh, oh…"

"That's okay."

"Okay, bye." She walked away.

I got back to work. For the first thirty minutes I felt funny. It was hard to focus. So, I had coffee. I looked over last night's work, then the morning's work, then got back to work. Later that day I made plans with the girl. She was away then, but Friday night we planned to get together. Well, I never thought that something like this would happen…

On Friday afternoon I heard the lady say something, but not in that peculiar kind of way. It sounded like she was in the hall, if not between the walls, and sounded loud. She was yelling. Someone else was in the hall too. Yes, I was in the apartment, and they were in the hall, the lady and someone else. He said, "Ma'am, ma'am, you did the right thing by calling us."

Then, after a moment, "It's only a leak. No, just the pipe, just dripping. Should be quick. All right."

Then suddenly there was a big rushing sound—of water. Followed by, "We need…Yes, the vacuum!"

And then, almost immediately, the fire alarms went off. I thought, great…

I saved everything on my laptop, then everything on there to a flash drive. Then I packed my laptop, the flash drive, and a few other valuables, some sentimental, into my backpack and got ready to evacuate. I opened the door, thunderstruck. Water was just gushing from pipes and pouring out of the lady's apartment, right across the hall from mine, and the hall was already flooded, basically like a river, just a very loud river. With all the alarms going off, the whole situation was *loud.* Her door was open, and though I could not see anything inside—just water streaming out of her apartment, from above the doorway, on either side, and on the floor—I could hear her yelling. She was telling someone, two firemen actually, about the orbs of light and the radiation and many other unusual things. They were working on the pipes, quietly amid the noise, but she kept going. Some neighbors casually poked their heads into the hallway. We asked about evacuating, and one fireman said that we did not have to. So, we went back inside, or at least I did, and then water started leaking into my apartment from under the door. A big puddle formed right in the entryway. I put down several towels, then considered the situation, everyone's indifference. It was almost shocking. I thought, what, is this common?

In a way, it worsened. The fire department arrived with a large vacuum, and they had to use a power outlet in my apartment to power the machine. With everything else that was happening, it was very, very loud. But I could still think, what is going on?

Finally, things settled down. The sun came in through the window. The puddle slowly cleared up, but there was still some water in the entryway, even when the girl came over that night. I say girl, but maybe she was older than I was, or maybe not, either way, she probably called me boy. Were we not? Would it have been better to call her gal and if she called me guy, or if gal was woman and guy was man? Well, when does a girl become a woman and a boy become a man? I think that it has to do with endurance, what one can endure, and not give up. In any case, a funky name would have been best.

We talked not so deeply—yet. Later, many ideas that came out on the spot, I wrote down and fit into the book. Then it got fancy. She is an actress; I, a writer. At some point I told her about the cleanse that I was doing, the lifestyle change that I had made, and that I finally felt pretty good. She thought that she should try it, stick with it, actually do it, yes. Then, in the morning, I added another ingredient to it. It was a supplement called diatomaceous earth, the fossils of an alga known as diatoms, which are composed of silica. There are two different types, or grades, of this substance. I got the food grade variety, of course. It has a very low percentage of silica, and it's safe to consume. I had read that it naturally gets rid of all the bad organisms living inside your body—when there is an overgrowth—that can cause many different internal problems. So, of course, I tried it.

I began noticing the effects immediately. I consumed diatomaceous earth every day, this fine, powdery material. It looks like wheat flour. Maybe it was the day after I first started taking it when I began noticing the effects. I mean, I felt incredibly sick, as though I had the flu or I was even sick from alcohol. I basically was, just much worse. These bad organisms like fungi living inside of me died all at once, and there was certainly an overgrowth, because when the die-off occurs, the fungi release the same toxins as alcohol. But this was a lot worse. It was so, so bad, and so hard to move. It lasted for several days, this wave of sickness, and I wrote the hardest chapter in the middle of it—the King Sisyphus chapter. Then just as I patted myself on the back—for writing the chapter in a day while enduring the sickness—I got an awful rash all over my chest. This is another symptom of those internal organisms dying off—forming a rash. My body must have been so overpopulated with them, fungi, toxins, pathogens, all causing much of the suffering in the past, and at that moment, so much more. But that was a good sign. The rash meant that things were getting better, my body was fighting back. And I soon learned that, after enduring it, you get the reward. You feel "normal." But after putting up with it, all of it, for so long, what most people would consider feeling normal, you feel incredible. But I was not there yet.

First I had to endure the rash… It started off typically, I suppose, though I do not recall getting anything like it before. Then the rash worsened. After only a few days, it looked almost like a burn of some degree. Aw, it itched, it was awful, all over my chest. For a couple of weeks, it kept getting worse and it spread. I tried to alleviate it with some over-the-counter remedies. This gel-like ointment that I rubbed on the rash did not do much, other than alleviate the itch, but there was nothing else I had found that would help it. Maybe it itched less, but it continued to expand.

Then, my body just completely exhausted itself, trying to heal, feel normal, and reach an equilibrium, after all that time with dysbiosis.

For a day or two, the rash seemed to be, maybe, getting better. But then one morning…

It started as an ache around my lower right abdomen. It felt almost like something was obstructing my intestine. There was a lot of pressure. But I was used to that feeling already; it was like the discomfort. So I thought nothing of it at first. Before this, it had mostly been on the other side of my abdomen and always felt much lighter. Then it became more intense. I tried taking another shower. They always relax me. But this time it got worse and worse. It was, seriously, hurting. I got out of the shower and lay down on my bed, same thing. Sat in my study, still the same. An hour passed. I was sweating, I wanted to cry. I could not endure the pain any longer. I felt ashamed having to do it, I tried waiting it out, but it only got worse, I thought of the diatomaceous earth, then that I might be dying, so I called 911. First responders came fast. I must have looked troubled. They asked me on a scale of one to ten—that whole measurement of pain. But it was the up there with the worst. I could hardly walk. Sitting down was not better, nor standing still, lying down, nothing. I was worried. The ambulance ride was painful, long, bumpy, and maybe every time that we bounced, we lost a minute, traffic was that bad, and so was the timing. The hospital—Hollywood Presbyterian Medical Center—was only about two miles away. But it took over twenty minutes to get there—in an ambulance. Then we went inside and the emergency room was pretty empty, not busy. I staggered across the floor, then fell. The first responders checked me in. It was very nice of them to do that. They pretty much waited there with me, just around the corner and down the hall, as I vomited several times from the pain, crawling on the floor of the waiting room alone, nurses, doctors, people, patients, looking, but not saying anything.

Reaching, reaching, reaching for a hand, but there was no hand to hold.

Every second that passed was unbearable. I did not think that I could endure it any longer. It took I don't know how long, over an hour, to finally hear my name called. I went down the hall. I passed the first responders. Said, "Thank you..." I was groaning. They seemed sympathetic. They knew that I was in pain. They just did not know what it was. My vital signs had been "normal." They said, "You're not dying." It just felt like I was. I thought, how am I still alive as it is?

The medical center, or just this part of the emergency room that I was in, did not have any private rooms. There were many chairs, and each chair was separated by curtains that were made of thick fabric and hung from the ceiling. Our chairs were set up almost in the main hallway, just off to the side, and the curtains gave us patients sitting right next to each other at least a little privacy. My chair was next to the hallway, and luckily, it was right beside what seemed to be the head nurse's station.

We talked. Or at least I tried to. I answered some questions, groaning. Then I continued waiting. The nurses attended to the patients who were the loudest, some shouting and crying. I wanted to curse at the pain too, but I just could not do it. So, another hour passed. Barely conscious.

At some point I heard the nurse say, "24-year-old male with severe abdominal pain, right side. Says it feels like being stabbed. It was an eight. No, not the worst. He has an extensive medical history. I feel really bad. Yes, several hours ago..."

Then the nurse came back. "We're really sorry you had to wait so long..."

I sat slouched in the chair and could not move.

"How do you feel now?"

"Unhh..."

Then, suddenly, there was an IV beside my chair, and the nurse poked a needle into my arm. Something went wrong and blood squirted out of the needle. Maybe it was not connected to the tube. My shorts were stained. Tried again, it worked. Soon a dose of morphine entered my bloodstream. It was the most spectacular feeling, after all that time, the pain was gone!

A few minutes passed. One of the patients sitting next to me, behind the curtain, asked, "What are you in for?"

"I don't know yet," I said. "I was in some pain."

"Yeah, I saw you out there in the waiting room…"

Next, I got a CT scan. But it took at least an hour or two for the doctor to review it. Then the pain came back, almost as strong as before, so the nurse administered another dose of morphine. I liked this substance then, at that moment, not only because it completely masked the pain, but it also made me feel a bit giddy. It was probably destroying all the good organisms in my body, disrupting the flora, the equilibrium, making the whole problem worse, but I did not mind. The nurse and I talked for a while. A couple of other nurses came over and talked. Maybe it was interesting.

At last, the doctor came over and told me that I had kidney stones. Big stones, and some had just passed into my bladder, which can cause such intense pain.

"Congratulations." She smiled, then said, "It's worse than childbirth."

"Thank you…" I signed some papers, got up, and left the hospital.

Chapter 40

How to go about making this chapter, and possibly the one after, then the end of part two?

There were many instances that night after leaving the hospital of trying to figure out what that whole experience meant, and means, going through it alone.

In the morning, I relieved myself and the small stones from my bladder. The most interesting thing about the stones was that a couple of them almost had fractal-like formations, and I had just written about fractals in the book, in *Any Moment*. I thought, what a coincidence. Then, the most frustrating or surprising thing about the experience, I learned later, was the hospital bill—for $13,000. I thought about all the people who were treated before me, or rather instead of me, and how it all seemed, their bills were likely for much less... That was damaging. I had kidney stones, it was excruciating, but the stones passed on their own. I just needed that pain medication.

The bill was really to just, wait around in the emergency room, in terrible pain, being ignored, and then after several hours of waiting, finally receiving pain medication, and then talking to the staff and other patients, and after waiting for several more hours, speaking to the doctor for only a moment—that was it, the bill. If anything, they might have gotten more out of their day by my being there that time than if this misfortune hadn't happened and I continued working on the book instead. But I was there, and that all happened; the book was waiting.

I did not even think about all that until after completing the book because I was so focused on everything, determined to finish the book, and then get the reward. I thought that maybe if students studied it, and libraries and schools carried several copies of it, that would be good. Every year schools require students to study books, passages, texts, and I thought that book and many of its passages and texts are applicable to them, the next generation, or past, or future. Sometimes all that you need is to read the right text or hear the right talk to know what to think, spark the next idea, make a big change. But please give credit. A lot of time, energy, self, and much more went into it. It does not necessarily matter what books or texts students study, what they read for leisure, or anyone else. If a studio or publisher were to buy it, instead of letting others profit from it, thank you. I could query again and try for that. But I told myself to wait until after finishing the project and after figuring out the problems, then after moving in. "One project at a time, one problem at a time," not knowing that while moving several problems would arise, causing a nexus of problems as well. And just as I started figuring out the problems, just as everything started getting better the big event, it all got much worse after.

As soon as I got home from the hospital, I got back to work. At that time, the book was the project, and the discomforts were the problem. Both were coming together, and both required separate efforts to, finish one, then figure out the other. But they were both difficult to do, especially at that same time.

I wrote a lot, of course, and I also learned a lot about the discomforts, what causes them, the root cause or causes themselves, and what helps. Later I saw or imagined it, all of it, differently too. Imagine I or my body as the world, the earth. All of the organisms together, especially once there was an overgrowth, started draining me. Then diatomaceous earth was introduced, fungi and bacteria died off, but it was harsh for some time. Then there was a big event, the time in the hospital, the worry, then the discovery, and then an equilibrium. I found out or rather discovered what the problem was. Then, things got much better, and from the inside, most bodily problems corrected themselves. The body needs an equilibrium and so does the world, the earth.

It first started with aloe vera juice; though I continued writing through the discomforts for a little while after going to the hospital. Then I tried the aloe vera juice—I had learned that it can ease inflammation, pain inside *and* outside of the body. After the first small glass, my stomach felt better, less inflamed, irritated. I felt better, had more clarity. Oh, it was different to write, maybe easier, but different. And I continued drinking aloe vera juice, often from a glass with ice, as I wrote and learned more about the discomforts.

My body, or really my kidney, could not tolerate the cleanse, riding it of sugars, starches, what fueled the overgrowth, and then consuming the earth, what balanced the overgrowth. It produced many toxins, and there were likely more that were already present, making an excess of toxins, but the body mostly filters out toxins through urine or sweat. At that time, I hardly sweat other than while getting exercise, so most of the toxins during the cleanse apparently had only one way out of my body, through urine, and there were so many toxins causing such an imbalance that my kidney could not filter out everything. Then, the stones formed.

Before that happened, or maybe as it was happening, on the night of the flood when the girl came over she had told me to go in saunas more often—as we were talking about cleanses. She said that after an hour, the towel that she was sitting on was all dirty, that's how many toxins she had sweat out. I thought, oh...

So, I began going in saunas once a week, but that started after going to the hospital. I remembered sitting inside saunas often when I was younger, some with steam, and most were public, but I thought that the ones in town seemed better. They were private infrared saunas for one or two people, and they had a radio, music was played, and I sweat—but all the

135

toxins had already been excreted, had hardened first, turned to stone, then flushed out. And the horrible rash, right after drinking aloe vera juice, went away in two days. The only scar from that event is a small brown dot that was not there before right next to a scar that was.

What was left were the abdominal discomforts, and though they felt at least somewhat relieved after drinking the juice and sitting in the sauna, my stomach still felt irritated. Something was still causing this to happen, the stomach pain. Then I learned what it was, and it all started coming together.

Chapter 41

I first learned about an acronym called FODMAPs, which I will explain the meaning of in a moment. In a way, it is a group of foods that all share a similar composition, and though the foods are all different, they are found in more or less every food group. These foods all contain certain sugars that, for some people, when broken down, the small intestine has trouble absorbing. Eating foods that are high in these sugars, or high in FODMAPs, will cause abdominal pain, distension, irritation, yes, but it also causes pain to the mind, stress to reason. It adds tolerance to pain. And this is my hypothesis, or that's the reason for it, being inside of a department store after hours. That is described in the first book, *The One*. And as of right now, as I'm writing this book, it's still on my record. But the court didn't know all this, or everything else.

That event or the arrest balanced my mind, almost as the cleanse or the earth balanced my body, and I noticed this right after. But while that event was taking place, and also for a little while leading up to it, the stomach discomfort was more pronounced than it had been before; I was 19, and that's all the time before then. The discomfort was acute even, and there is a direct brain-gut connection.

I'm thinking now about that arrest, and the big event in New Orleans, comparing the two. I did not cause damages, get past security codes, locked doors, or devices. But I was arrested and went through the system. Yet people harmed and caused damages to me; someone stole my debit card, made absurd purchases; someone stole my cell phone, got past the passcode, stole money; assets; and someone else, but not that night, apparently got into my locked car, either inside of a locked lot or garage, then caused damages to the car and to me; and nothing happens to any of them. Whereas I suffer.

In any event, getting back to the condition, the acronym FODMAPs stands for fermentable oligosaccharides, disaccharides, monosaccharides, and polyols. They are all sugars that some people, their digestive system, cannot absorb. These sugars are found in many different foods. The worst, and these might be the worst because as ingredients they are added to so many foods, meals, recipes, are onions and garlic. That includes the actual vegetables, their powders, flavors, or any other forms derived from either. It's not that they are worse than other foods high in FODMAPs, though both are highly concentrated in F, they are just commonly used. But, there are many other common foods that contain those kinds of sugars, all kinds of fruits, vegetables, grains, dairy, and more.

Sadly, I learned that avocados are high in one of the sugars. Not all foods that are high in FODMAPs will cause a reaction, but find out what does and make modifications.

It was simple, really, figuring this out, that I've always had and now really have at least a touch of I-B-S. And to still go on, still perform well, that's good. Apparently, this condition is more common for females to experience, but males can too, and gods. It's not a bad bowel; it can just be sensitive, mostly to those sugars.

Well, after diagnosing this condition, that was when I received the hospital bill. One minute and a few words with the doctor cost thousands of dollars. I thought, wow, if only I had found out this condition sooner, and everything else had been better. That would've been nice...

Chapter 42

Not long after the hospital visit, passing the stones, and then figuring out the condition, the infection cleared up, yellow toenails went away. They had grown out normally, starting right after the hospital visit, after consuming the earth. No longer wearing socks. The dermatitis was gone.

It is ironic that I have trouble absorbing certain sugars, yet sugars were fueling the fungal infection. I do not know if the fungal infection caused the abnormal bowel condition, if the condition caused the infection, or if they were both there from birth, or both worsened because of everything else—both being part of that first world, and both being internal problems, which led to all of these worlds, and some of these problems.

I also figured out, after deciding to move because of the pandemic, it was not that I was unhappy, it was because of the infection, the irritation, not knowing the condition, what causes the discomforts, the insecurities. These issues just had to get figured out.

With the discomforts mostly relieved, the rest of the book might have been easier to write, but it really felt better to write. It was getting close to the end of that book; I was getting eager to finish it. I had big plans after, an adventure, and I was excited and healthy and ready and feeling good, maybe better than any time before.

I still ran, of course. I had found a different route about a week after going to the hospital and enduring the stones. God knew that I had trouble sleeping because of the discomforts, especially during that time, so after working on the book through the evening and into the night, I went on a run at midnight three or four times a week. Even then I was getting eager, and after learning about the condition and then easing the discomforts, running too felt better. Everything felt better. The runs, or the routes, were not as straightforward as going around Whitley Heights; these went through the Hollywood Dell!

I lived by the two historic neighborhoods, and the first time that I went to the latter on foot, it was to have breakfast, and the journey there was awesome. The route running through the Hollywood Dell and further up the ridge was arduous, half of it at least, which was mostly uphill. I started going often to prepare for hiking Mt. Whitney, the tallest mountain in the continental United States. After figuring out the problems, and after finishing the book, that was the plan, the first adventure.

Just going on these runs was an adventure, and because the main route was quite complex, going through it felt different every time. This is important. A new idea formed or association was made.

These runs really started after crossing street, picking up speed, up a slight grade, going through a tunnel underneath the overpass. I turned and went down a terrace, passed a temple, and went left up Vine toward the hills, the sign. There was a small cul-de-sac on the right side a little ways down the street with a stairway that led up to another street, another adventure, another idea. Then there was the hill, a steep hill, one that even walking up uses muscle, running up takes courage.

At the top of it, for the next mile or two, it went uphill, but beautifully uphill, with views of the city, the lights at night, downtown and all around. That was following a turn, going around a corner where for a moment the view opened up. The street at that point was concrete, uneven and cracked. Under the moon it was more of a thrill. Unable to really see the pavement, with all the large breaks and rifts, being alert was necessary. After working on everything, having to focus, that helped. I had heard that there might be coyotes in the area;

maybe there were, watching me, as I was watching myself in you, the city.

There was a short climb to the top of the ridge, going past a garden, all of its sculptures, then along the ridge a little way leading up to the neighborhood lake. Here I went right, down the ridge toward the canyon. At the bottom of the street there was another, different, garden. It was gated off at least at night, but facing the road right outside of the gate was a throne that I sometimes sat in, my only break. The plan was to hike Mt. Whitney in a day, so there would be very few breaks, crampons required, I had to be in good shape. And I was. I felt great—especially in that throne, with the stars, under the moon. From there, it was a pleasant, steady run going south through the canyon. There was the intersection and a café on the corner with a stone archway built over the sidewalk and underneath were shelves and books and some day, I thought, maybe mine will be there.

One time, after going through the archway and continuing down the road, this idea for a movie came to mind. The scene starts with a view of the Hollywood Sign from inside a car driving up Wilcox, approaching Franklin. There is a red light at the intersection, but before having to stop the car, the light turns green, the car goes through, then gets hit, rolls over. The camera lands on the ground, still focused on the sign. A few people go by, their legs, feet, hurriedly. Someone picks up the camera and through the lens the car is inverted, there are people crowding around it, but the driver is gone.

Chapter 43

I did not finish the book in time to hike Mt. Whitney. I had bought a day permit when they were still available, but it was only valid for that particular day, and I was still working on the book that day but after finishing it there were no permits available, I believe for the rest of the season. It was upsetting, on that particular day, not going on that adventure. But the book was coming together well, it was nearly done, and that was exciting. As soon as I finished it, I sent a proof copy to someone who I admired and viewed like a father. Then I got some gear, filled up The Honda, and went to Big Sur!

I arrived just after noon and drove up the ridge in Plaskett. I found a spot high above the fog and it was the first one with a great view. Then I set up the area, before rightly taking it in.

Nothing can describe this view—right now. I have taken pictures and videos but they do not capture the feeling, free of discomforts, a heavenly feeling. I am above the clouds somewhere along a mountain ridge. It is probably 70 degrees Fahrenheit and sunny. There are no clouds in the sky around or behind me, but far out there below me it is substantially cloudy. I am facing the ocean, and all along the coast in both directions are points of land part of ridges, mountains, jutting out into the sea, but hovering above the sea is a seemingly infinite layer of fog. Directly ahead, in every direction, it all looks like snow, a whole frontier of it, but it is warm. There are pine trees all around, rolling hills, mountain peaks. I cannot wait for the fog to dissipate, so all that is visible, with the rest of the view, is perfect blue. Let's go explore.

Part 3

The Unusual Conclusion

Chapter 44

Shortly after all the problems arose that one night in New Orleans and after, as I was waiting for a resolution, it was necessary to write an essay to Bank of America, and the essay is essential to the book, and the book is being written for them. Word for word, this is it:

To Whom It May Concern:

It is upsetting that after all this time since the fraudulent activity took place, after speaking with several agents from the fraud department and retelling the same story repeatedly, that I now must write out the story because after the investigation took place, the fraud department was unable to approve my recent claim and pay me back.

So, here is the story once again—from me in writing. That way I do not waste any more time trying to get back the money that was stolen from me. I do not want to have to do this, but to me it was a lot of money, and a serious event.

It happened on 06/29/2021 – 06/30/2021 while I was moving long distance to another state. I had to stay overnight in four different states, five different cities, and the night of June 29 was in New Orleans, Louisiana.

I wanted to experience the city, particularly the French Quarter, as much as I could in one night. I had been driving all day; that night I went out. I had some food, some drinks, a good time. Then, at some point, I reached into my pocket and my cell phone was gone, then I checked my wallet and my debit card was gone.

I believe, after learning about the area, that I got pickpocketed and that it was probably the same person who stole my cell phone who also stole my debit card. I knew that in the morning I would have to call Bank of America to report my lost debit card, but also that it might be a bit tricky because after all I did not have my cell phone, which meant that I would have to call Apple and seek their advice on the situation.

Then, this is where the situation really became a problem, and a very tricky one. Overnight my car died—for reasons that are not relevant to this paper, or essay rather, but are interesting and alarming nonetheless—so in the morning my plans got changed. I first called Honda roadside support, to get my car towed and back on the road again, because I was moving long distance and had to keep my schedule for the move-in date. To place the call, I used the hotel's landline phone, and Honda support said that a tow truck would arrive in one hour. While waiting in the lobby, next I called Apple, because not having a cell phone was almost the most bothersome part about the whole experience—so far.

Long story short, we tried using the Find My Phone app on my laptop but I was locked out of iCloud and could not reset my password because a verification code had to be sent to my phone but I did not have my phone and that was the only way to verify myself. Then, while we were trying to figure out another way to get access to my iCloud account, I got an email on my laptop letting me know that the Find My Phone app had been disabled—from my cell phone. That was when I learned that someone had actually gotten inside my cell phone and they were using it. Even at first, early on, it was scary! So, the Apple support agent suggested that I disable my cell phone. And I tried to. I called Spectrum next because service providers are the only entities able to disable a cell phone, and while I was on the phone with them having a hard time of course getting verified, the tow truck arrived and I had to hang up and go to the dealership.

Because I did not have a cell phone, I had to put calling Bank of America about my missing debit card, and calling Spectrum about disabling my cell phone, on hold. I spent the whole day at the garage waiting for my car, unable to attend the other problems, and though it is not relevant, my car did not even get fixed that day, it only got me to where I was moving to. Anyway, after finally getting back to the hotel, I made my rental payment because it was due by 5:00pm that afternoon. If I failed to do so, the landlord said that I would not be able to move in. But I made the payment just in time—from my laptop. Then two minutes later I received the first of several unnerving emails—from Coinbase.

They were basically all confirmation emails, confirming several transactions made on Coinbase from my cell phone. The person who had stollen my cell phone and then got inside of it, and I mean they must have hacked past the six-digit security code because no one would have been able to figure it out, then they got onto Coinbase because the Coinbase app requires no additional security to open the app once the cell phone is being used, and then they initiated these transactions, seemingly emptying my checking account which was linked to my Coinbase account. It was frightening, getting those emails, seeing confirmation transactions for thousands of dollars, seeing money just go like that.

Then, after thinking for a moment, I called Bank of America first. I had a very hard time getting into my account, because like Apple, I needed to verify myself by getting a code sent to my cell phone. But I did not have a cell phone. It was difficult, it took a while, but finally the agent and I got into my account. That's when we saw the 30+ fraudulent transactions still in the processing stage.

Next thing I knew I was on the phone with the checking account fraud department. I cannot remember if the Coinbase transactions were actually showing up in the processing stage, or if they were not yet showing and the agent put a block on all future Coinbase transactions—to prevent the fraudulent activity on Coinbase from actually going through. Luckily, whatever the agent did, it worked. As of now the transactions never went through and after that they did not and do not appear on my bank statement. Coinbase, however, said that I still owed them all that money—because the transactions did in fact go through on their end, and whoever stole my cell phone and got into, sent the money from the transactions to themselves and they received it, I believe.

Here is some information that Coinbase sent in an email on the night of 06/30:

> Our records indicate that the transaction you reported as unauthorized was initiated from the IP 174.255.1.152 matching your geolocation, using your verified iOS device.
>
> We understand that your account may have been compromised and unauthorized activity occurred. Please note you are solely responsible for the security of your devices, email, passwords, and 2FA codes. Using these compromised credentials, they were able to initiate the following external send:
>
> 2021-06-30 1:56 PM PDT 0.05501517 BTC send to external address bc1q5wvlskmgte237rmzvqrd2n2qt4sn764zjqqpsp.
>
> 2021-06-30 1:41 PM PDT 0.02859414 BTC send to external address 3CsUEtJzGBK4fHuQ3i7R5nhXbi2ZUJjGt1.
>
> 2021-06-30 1:34 PM PDT 0.05437791 BTC send to external address 3CsUEtJzGBK4fHuQ3i7R5nhXbi2ZUJjGt1.

On Coinbase's end, not that it is very relevant, it shows that the time of the transactions occurred between 1:30

and 2:00pm. For me, when I received the confirmation emails on my laptop, it was between 4:30 and 5:00 pm. I think that this information might have something to do with the time zone. But, to get back to the real issue...

Later, they said, 'Please note, Coinbase is unable to reverse digital currency transactions, and we will not be able to recover these lost funds.'

Finally after going back and forth with them even more, I explained this whole story, and I have yet to hear back from them regarding the issue. I take it that they were just understanding about the whole situation, that the issue with them was resolved in a way, and that I do not owe them anything *because I am the victim here.*

Even so, I still spent a lot of time having to explain everything, and time cannot be repaid.

Originally, in the email, they said that I am responsible for my electronic devices. But I did not understand how I am responsible for someone reaching into my pocket without my knowing and stealing almost everything. All in all, it was a very stressful experience. And I mean just having to go back and forth with customer support—not much support, or care, it seemed.

Well, anyway, after working with the agent from Bank of America's checking account fraud department, I got transferred to the debit card fraud department. Those 30+ fraudulent transactions that were showing on my bank statement as processing, the debit card agent and I reviewed them and opened a claim for them. The most concerning transactions were from Cash App and Apple Cash. The person who stole my cell phone did the same thing with Cash App and Apple Cash as they did with Coinbase, but these transactions, though they were each of and all totaled less money, indeed went through, and they posted on my statement sometime later.

Also, I should note that when working with the agent, my debit card at the time ending in 4119 got deactivated and a new card ending in 9379 got issued. From my end, it appears right now that some of the transactions from Cash App and Apple Cash got processed and posted on the statement under the card ending in 4119 and some of those transactions got processed and posted under the card ending in 9379. Both cards got deactivated, of course. But two separate claims got opened because of this, one for the card ending in 4119 and one for the card ending in 9379. All of the fraudulent transactions occurred on either 06/29/2021, 06/30/2021 or 07/01/2021. On the statement, the ones that went through show 06/30, 07/01, 07/02. All this I learned sometime later as well.

That night, however, the agent and I went through each transaction one by one. He stated the transaction, where it was from and for how much it was of, and I said either "Yes it is fraudulent" or "No it is not fraudulent." This is where again it gets a bit tricky. I knew that I went out the previous night, even that I possibly used an atm for a $20 withdrawal, but I was unsure if I actually did, and like I said, I was also unsure exactly what time my phone and my debit card got stolen.

So... As I told the agent on the phone, I was positive that most of those transactions from that night were fraudulent, that they were done by whoever pickpocketed me. Like, the Cash App transactions, Apple Cash transactions, Melbas Wash World transactions, the Dollar Tree transaction, the Discount City transaction, McDonald's transaction, et cetera. But, I am not positive if the two ATM withdrawals from Solaris Gara-2610 each for $23.75 was me or the person who stole my debit card. This is the reason, an agent just told me, why my claim did not get approved and why I was unable to get back my money—because my debit card's pin number had to be used for an atm withdrawal and I said that I was the only one who knew the pin number. But when being unsure if just two minor transactions from an ATM were initiated by me or if they were fraudulent, if that gets the whole claim unapproved, that I just do not understand.

Well, I hope that all this helps the investigation team understand the whole situation and story a little more. That way, this time, the details that I included to one agent or another will not get lost in translation by the time they in fact make it to the team.

It was such a stressful move. I have lost quite a bit of money because of it, sleep too, and even possibly some hair. I certainly hope that this does not happen to someone else in the future, and that in my case, this claim or issue will get positively resolved.

Thank you,

Andrew Therriault

P.S. An agent with the fraud department also said that I must file a report with law enforcement to get my claim approved. Then, of course, there was another problem. I tried filing a report after arriving at and settling into my apartment, but the officer told me that I cannot file a report here because the crime did not occur here. And I cannot go back to New Orleans just to file the report, it costs too much money, takes too much time. So, I hope that the investigation team will be more than understanding regarding this issue. I have tried very hard just to get my money back, just to get a little peace of mind."

Chapter 45

After realizing that I used the verb got just a little too often, instead of the verbs was or were, because I used Grammarly for that paper, since I didn't expect to write a book about all of it, I had already sent the paper. Then, while waiting for a resolution and for my thumb to heal, I continued making notes, mostly unedited, those of a Sunday afternoon, 07/2021, continued...

"Strange how it works, the climate...

"Beware of this app, and that app! All of that fraudulent activity, money seemingly stolen, they're not insuring it. They decided that there was no fraudulent activity. Also, customer support was quite difficult, and whoever stole my cellphone and caused all of these problems, why did you do that to me? Now I might have to get surgery on my thumb...

"Nice, I finally have a place to sit and work. No nice views. Wobbly chairs. But it's a place to sit, have a wooden table, good. It's been three weeks here without a place to sit, a study, table for work. It should be easier now...

"I like the island. Maui has a similar climate. Oh, that'd be good to experience...

"Back in the emergency room... At least now I might be able to find out if I need surgery. Plus, I had some key lime pie earlier, still feel good...

"But I can't really make a note here, it's packed, and not like a packed place with beer and food and wine all around, people noisy maybe in joy. Though people here are noisy, it sounds like it's because of illness or pain. Bless the ER...

"Quick visit so far. Anyway, the only place indoors better than either of those places is a tranquil place…

"Other than that, it's probably outdoors in a nice place, and that could be anywhere, preferably being active and doing something, because that really gets the mind sparking…

"Good news, no surgery needed! That's what the doctor said, then that the thumb will heal on its own, but it takes time. Maybe the doctor was just intentionally brushing me off. But my fingers are crossed. Now, where was I?

"The sun is out today, and I'm still breathing, I'm not in pain, I'm smiling. I think I should have some takoyaki. It is too soon for a swim—my thumb, I don't know—but in my mind I can, from the day before I got the stitches, nice day that was…

"Why am I still waiting for a nurse? The stitches are out, might just go…

"Well, I should eat. It's 5:00pm and I'm still waiting at the hospital—for an X-ray…

"Still waiting. Now thinking, the new book should come together nicely, intricately, at least. It won't write itself. But I'm still here, and I need to eat after, perhaps… Perhaps… Coffee would be good…

"An x-ray should be straightforward. So, it shouldn't be much longer. Someone in the room next to me fell into a hole on the sidewalk, and now they're here, and they don't remember how they got here—what is anything?"

"I been going out for food and drink a lot lately? Maybe it's because for a year plus everything was closed, and everyone was inside. Although inside I am indeed in my element, work and fun can be done outside too. Writing notes, inside or outside, can happen anywhere. The one later is where, right now it's how…

"In line at the DMV, long line, probably a long wait. But, it seems to be moving. I wish I could get a coffee and wait here with it. My thumb looks funny, still swollen. I'm just glad that I still have it. But it is moving more, both the DMV line and my thumb...

"Maybe half the people in the mall right now are here at the DMV. I still can't believe that I had a big piece of ceramic sticking out of my thumb that night, almost two weeks ago...

"As for the Other night, I have no idea. I'm still recovering from that. Hopefully my quick paper faxed to Bank of America will help me get a positive resolution—with everything. And a real investigation takes place. What an overall bad experience, especially in the aftermath of That night—so far. Come on Edward from Cash App support. The light that you shed is very dim... I'm at the DMV right now and I just got your email. Some of these financial institutions can be problematic. Maybe my "economic theories of change," or something like that, would actually work, if I got an advance to write a paper on how to implement them...

"Frustrating email replying to Edward from Cash App support. Knowing how things have gone with support agents as of late, he probably won't see it, it'll probably be someone else that does...

"My eyesight has always been good, perfect. Now it is apparently getting worse, probably from using close range vision so much, almost like a scientist...

"First I wanted to write a book, that was my goal. Then that turned into multiple books, five written, three still published, and working on another. Started writing these notes for it, but what will it and these notes turn into? Eyesight was good, but I can never foresee these things...

"Good news, my new license picture looks better than the last one. In that one I looked older and more stressed. Maybe I was, maybe that means things will get better, depending on all of this...

"Oh, these notes just add up... But... how to make something from them, or this, writing, Art? Maybe, start designing buildings, grand structures, blueprints, like a kind of castle, for everyone...

"Would investors or managers or banks be on board? Maybe someone or some entity would. Definitely a kind of ambassador would…"

"Wow, randomly at this quiet bar many many miles away two college kids that both go to the colleges I went to just sat next to me. They seemed a bit surprised at the stories that I told them, or at least to them they were different. Still, though it happened several years later, I ask why do that to me and my car, my cell phone, and everything else?

"I know that these notes might seem repetitive, but they are just notes, you know I'm just trying to help myself, during a very difficult time, that's the only explanation I have for the past, everything else…

"Anyway, after talking to those college kids, and seeing them now, it seems like some kids these days are addicted to gambling. I wonder what the other things are, for other kids? Or maybe not kids. Maybe a form of media, but it's always changing, like some climates…

"I write these notes on the go, like a painter with a portable easel…

"That college student said that he knew insider trading, though it seemed more like gambling, something about a person who had streaked in the super bowl, they might have known the person, maybe it altered the game and the online casino found out and blocked all bets and winnings and losses from going through. Now that's good customer support…

"It's raining outside, nice. Takoyaki that means, great. It's just a weather change, it all smells good…

"Big Sur smelled good too. And I'm sure Maui does…

"Wish I could say hey, let's talk. I need someone to go out with right now, these tourists just… I don't know… I could talk to you; I should learn from you, and you should learn from me. Writing is hardly part of the experience, but supplemental; in time, a lot will be learned. I wish we could just talk, even eat, some good food, et cetera. And maybe do a lot more for the world too…

"In any case, party tonight…

"Now… That really is what it is…

"Yes, I might be smart, I might be able to paint the bigger picture, but…

There's everything else that I enjoy, and everything else that makes, makes everyone feel good, too…"

"It gets rough out there…

"I just examined the FL driver's license that I received today. Registered at the DMV, using my previous driver's license. Why the person issued me a "Class E" "Learner's License," I have an idea. Clearly my driver's license said "Driver's License" "Class C." Why are people giving me a hard time? Didn't ask for that, after everything, didn't even ask to be born. Now I'll have to go back and wait again at the DMV and explain this situation, then hope that things can just be right for once, not rough…

"Well, at least the move to CA and the move in CA went pretty smoothly, for the most part. But then when something did go wrong, though it was a long drive, I had a place to stay for the weekend, and both times people were good. This time the move did not go smoothly, not as good…

"Only thinking about the bad experiences, but I've had many more than usual in FL since moving…

"These experiences are starting to seem personal. They always have, now that I think about it. And there have been a lot…

"This is why lawyers are helpful, seems like I'm becoming my own lawyer, for things that are not my fault, and I don't get paid for it. Just lose time, energy, get knocked down, what. Just keep going, keep going, yes…

"Oh, writing it down now. The person at the DMV was of course, sassy, but it's a DMV what do you expect, well, after getting the learner's license she clipped and threw away my driver's license. If I now have trouble getting an actual driver's license because I was issued a learner's license and I have no real driver's license anymore, I might just give up…

155

"Nothing is going right…

"Taking a fourth driving test would do it…

"Like symbolism…

"Ah and I can't fall asleep or even relax right now. All these problems have really knocked me down…

"I can handle other people's problems, but when they're mine and I get knocked down it's just much more, or even, just worse…

"Here's a good motto, look both ways before crossing the road. And the driver's license will be figured out. The thing is—nothing to do with the driver's license—I do a lot of notes in times of distress, it levels everything, I feel better. Then I go out more, day and night, and I enjoy that. These ideas I would never think of just sitting at the MacBook. Or in a study, but not necessarily. That could be anywhere, but I also get different ideas doing different things. Hiking will be different from biking, running, walking, talking, jogging, et cetera… It's probably true for every activity, anywhere in the world, in any world…"

Chapter 46

Sunday 07-25-2021

"Maybe creation should start over. Think, human population back down to 100, or 1,000, or 10,000, 100,000, let them rebuild creation—into this again, taking several million years, or into something completely different. Maybe in "their" world there would be no wars, conflicts, long waits, disputes. Maybe it would be worse, more of the above, or maybe there would be much more kindness, love, generosity, forgiveness. Maybe "our" planet would in a way thank us, and then have time to regenerate what resources we have taken from "her," or "here." There's not much of a difference, it's mother earth, and it probably takes energy. Meanwhile, maybe other resources, other elements and compounds that do not yet exist, would then be created. Maybe the populace would form a different or even a better kind of society. The world rotates automatically. The cube does not, but systematically. This is all what creation, not evolution or adaptation, does."

"This is all just a quick note of course, an unprompted idea. But to actually recreate like that, in a way, would probably be very good. Plus, I got two yolks in my egg this morning."

"It's a Sunday though, why think about this right now? Why not think about something maybe more expected, sex? I do, but all these events, and (my thumb)."

"Sunday morning thought... Laundry... It's been almost two weeks without a clean shirt because of my thumb. So, don't wear one..."

"How else would the populace go from 10,000 to 7-8,000,000,000 so fast? Once upon a time there was little to no clothing in society."

"When *someone* takes my ideas without giving credit or compensation, or when someone else actually takes my, notes, without my knowing, a person in distress can only take so much, and that's when the pearl emerges. But in all forms, just a loving part of creation."

"Ending thought, for now: I did not ask to be born, to have to deal with these problems, and these problems date back to when I was born, I am just present, and that is creation..."

"This Friday I should really go to that event."

"And this coming week, after I finally make it to the beach of a Key, see the botanical garden, paddle board, do a few things that I would've liked to do but could not do because of my thumb, though my thumb still feels radically wrong, after that, maybe just a day more, I will really sit down and get to work, especially on the book-in-progress."

"I have not really felt good, ever. I hope that these issues with the bank, and the other issues from that night and throughout my life, see a positive resolution."

"Aside from everything else, right now it's all right, in this moment. I right now am all right, in this moment. But... Where would everyone else go? Somewhere else, and let those here continue creation."

"When the time comes, the mind will be ready. Because down to the organ, not the accordion, that is what creation, existence, is..."

"It's interesting, people everywhere are different, not one and the same, but similar. I noticed as of late, after the big event occurred a few weeks ago, it's been a little different. What that means, I don't know, it's just an observation, and it's been a difficult time. I'm just here, you're just here, we're all just part of creation. Why can't things be, just, good."

"But, that was just the observation. If anyone else had these experiences and they were still walking, talking, would they still like anything, everything, or even the sunrise?"

"These notes of a Sunday afternoon—better than the last thread. Maybe, they're just unprompted notes of a thread, of a Sunday afternoon."

"Notetaking is like fishing, but instead of trying to catch fish from the water, it's trying to describe ideas from the mind. Some fishhooks or lures will attract certain fish while fishing, and some prompts or questions will inspire certain ideas while notetaking. All the notes that I've taken have been unprompted, like going fishing with just a hook. Yet I've recorded some good ideas. They would've been good fish, if I'd been fishing, with just a hook. But if I had prompts to help inspire notes, and if I had a good spot to try and get them down, that would be great."

"Do I think that these things, these problems, sufferings all throughout time just happened by chance? Not in reflection. But come on."

"Like a good resolution."

"I believe that few other people would have been able to navigate through all those problems at once, so if they can't they're then likely able to sue for damages, but because I could, I can't, other than that it all caused incredible pain and distress, so why should I suffer more for being able to, endure much more, finesse the rest, and why should they be rewarded?"

"So, I just learned… Onions alone do not hurt my stomach too much. But they do, a lot. That has nothing to do with a resolution; it's gotten worse because of no resolution, so far, for anything. It is only an observation, and it means right now I must follow and stick to the dietary changes."

"I think that something is seriously wrong with my thumb. It could be worse, but this is just frustrating, I cannot even open a packet of mayonnaise in my own home. I'm going to bed."

"Up early, 5:30am, just to go back to the DMV at 7:00am. Hopefully it goes well and I get what should have been issued after waiting for four hours on Friday, a Class C driver's license. That memory just sprouted up—huh, interesting"

"This is ridiculous. It's 7:00am and the line is longer than it was on Friday, mid-day."

"At least I got to skip the line. That was a good person, could tell that I was a bit frustrated."

"I had to take the picture again and it looks worse than the picture on Friday, ha-ha. I look a bit stressed again, wonder why…"

"Some coffee will help, and the idea of waking up at 5:00am every day and going for a run then, instead of at midnight, is good. Will I be able to do that, why not? That's too early, that's why."

"It is 07/27/2021. Sunrise was nice. Day started all right, I finally made it to the beach of a Key, then I got an email from the landlord. Who was the one who took a picture of the box by the recycling bins that I could not break down because I had a dozen stitches in my hand? Then complained to the landlord, who then charged me a fee because of it?"

"What is anything?"

"Was right about that app. A different agent saw and responded to the last email. Nothing new, still no resolution, still locked out of my account. Same issue with another app, and more. Bad things happen, and whatever happened to me was beyond unfortunate. But because it did happen to me, that means that it could happen to anyone. And thousands of dollars from one account could be millions or more from something else…"

"Now 08/02. What is even worse, the bank lost the paper that I faxed them. Different agents, having to explain the same story, taking more time, energy. So much stress, frustration, inconvenience. And then, the fraud claim was disapproved and they took away the temporary credit. This is ridiculous, yes. More so, serious. How will I be compensated for all this?"

"Anyway, as for the serious event... That night in New Orleans is starting to feel like that night in New Hampshire, at UNH. Memories from even before that night, both nights, are fogged up, strange, hard to discern."

"Well, notes are great. I love writing them. But this book won't write itself."

"What time is it?"

"Yes."

Chapter 47

Everything in this chapter happened, and over a few days one experience after another felt like, another déjà vu. They were similar to some experiences that had happened before, but instead of occurring far apart in time, these happened almost all at once.

I finished writing the book in early September, and I had to wait to write this chapter until after getting an MRI for my thumb and then having a doctor's appointment and finding out about the results. It took that long to see the hand doctor; the soonest available appointment was almost two months after the stitches were taken out.

Shortly after that, about a month and a half ago, was when an agent from the bank told me that they lost the paper that I had faxed them. Then I sent it again and said that I was going to write a book based on or around the event and then the experience afterward, because I was and I am very displeased, and pained. Then that idea of what it would be turned into this; it is interesting how the mind will try to solve a problem.

Also, the thumb injury made it hard to do anything else, and as I write this right now, that is still the case. The injury was a good reason to write; I cannot grip anything with my left hand or even move my thumb much at all. It is almost like being one-handed.

Even though the injury made it easier to sit down and write, it was still very hard writing this book. Working on the last one, *Any Moment*, I had things to look forward to. But working on this one, through all the problems, and everything else, I had the doctor's appointment to look forward to...

That happened on 09/15/2021, and some things happened leading up to it that were, unfortunate. I have documentation for all of it. On 09/10, I finished going through the book. I noticed a few typos, here and there on the page. But I kept some as is, just as a painter might leave an unintentional mark as is, on the canvas.

I finished going through the book maybe an hour or two after midnight. I spent all day just going through it, at many different places, but all nearby. Then I woke up at around 6:00am with some abdominal pain. For a couple of hours. the intensity stayed the same. Then it gradually started getting worse. At around 9:00am I knew what it was. I thought that I could wait it out, but at 10:00am it was bad, and for the next several hours it got worse. Just before noon I called 911 because I could not drive to the hospital. On 09/11/2021, I passed some stones again.

It was a *long* day. Somehow I took notes, which I hadn't really done since starting the book. They definitely showed the affliction. I did not go to the hospital first. I went to an urgent care clinic because it was closer and it was thought that I would get medical attention sooner.

I wrote, "They won't even give me any pain medication which is the reason why I came here. My hands are all tingly I'm vomiting tunnel vision I might faint."

I was groaning and they kept telling me to calm down, even getting upset. I asked, "Have you ever had kidney stones before?"

A security guard said, "I have. It, is, horrible."

Soon after that I went to the hospital. I was in the emergency room and even with morphine the pain was worse than the first time without it. It came in waves and when a wave hit it was too strong to think, and when it retreated, I thought, what will the bill be?

Just to get the stitches taken out, the bill was $1,200. I have no idea about this one, after having to get a CT scan and taking morphine, and it was kind of upsetting because I knew what it was and that's what I needed, but why did the morphine not have an effect?

I wrote, "Aw, no one is here with me. That nurse was, a second ago. But it'd be more endurable if I had, a hand."

The notes were very mellow compared to the pain experienced. The next day I went for a long run to clear my mind. I had found a good route or loop that I like to go on, and around. The following day was uneventful, and the day after was busy. That night I went on another run. Afterward I got a bottle of water from The Honda. Then I started the car, the engine turned on, and so did the power. Everything was good. I felt a cool draft from the air conditioner, then got out and went inside, and later, went to bed.

In the morning, I had the doctor's appointment for my thumb. I tried starting the car and the power turned on, but the engine did not. Then I tried shutting the car off, and the power shut off for a second, everything was off for a second. Then, without doing or touching anything else, the power, and only the power, turned back on. The same thing happened over and again, every time that I tried shutting the car off, it turned back on—on its own. Once I first turned the car on, it would not shut off after.

I still made it to the appointment on time, and when I got home, after being at the doctor's office for a few hours, the car had to be towed to the dealership. I could not believe that it was potentially happening again. They did not find any aftermarket parts, wires or devices this time. They only had to change the battery, and as far as I know, the car was not tampered with, again.

As for the appointment…

The doctor reviewed the MRI. My FPL tendon is torn and there is damage to the digital nerve. They will both need to be surgically repaired—if I'd ever like holding anything in my left hand again.

Thinking about the iceberg theory—four days earlier I thought of a book and one of the scenes in a hospital and then the dialogue of the one called Job, but sounds like Jobe, and was similar to, "Where are you, Job?" "Where are you, Job?" "Job, where are you?" And then, in a different voice, "Job, where is the driver?"

Afterward

It is 09/19/2021, three days before the book will be published, before one quarter turns to another. It is a Sunday, and the same issue is happening again with my car! I tried turning the car on and only the power turned on, the engine did not. Then I tried again and again, shutting the car off, and it shut off for one second and then, without doing anything else, without touching anything else, it immediately turned back on, but it will not shut off. I did not even turn the car on since the last time that it happened, less than a week ago, on 09/15, because I was afraid that something like it would happen again, and it did. Tried recording it on video, multiple times on my phone, and the videos kept stopping by themselves, but you see it first. It is as though the person who tampered with my car the first time completely messed it up, and now it just does not work properly. I have an idea of who it was, who might have made it happen, obviously. I've just been trying to live after all this suffering. Why did you do that with my phone in the first place? This is very serious, alarming. What happens next? I don't know.

Made in the USA
Columbia, SC
17 January 2023